Will The Time Ever Come?

A TLINGIT SOURCE BOOK

EDITED BY

Andrew Hope III and Thomas F. Thornton

DEDICATION

TO THE FOLLOWING CONFERENCE PARTICIPANTS
WHO HAVE PASSED ON:

Judson Brown, Shaakakoonee
Forrest DeWitt Jr., Káa Ch'áati
Matthew Fred, L.aangooshu
Austin Hammond, Daanawáak
Elizabeth Freda Hope, Tsanak / Taliiraq
Herb Hope, Stoonookw
John Hope, Kaalgeik'w
Ed Kasko, Suk.kees / Goosh Tlein
George Lewis, Saa.aat
Chris Makua, Gooch Éesh
Betsy McFarland, Neech'k
Maria Miller, Ldaneit
Elizabeth Nyman, Sedaya
Cooney Starr, Kalee.aan

ACKNOWLEDGMENTS

GRATEFUL ACKNOWLEDGMENTS TO THE FOLLOWING ORGANIZATIONS
THAT PROVIDED FUNDING FOR THIS PUBLICATION:

Alaska Native Knowledge Network/Center for Cross Cultural Studies
ANB Camp #2 (Juneau), Klukwan Heritage Foundation
Klukwan, Inc., Shee Atiká, Inc., Sitka Moose Club
Sitka Sound Seafoods, Sitka Tribe of Alaska
University of Alaska Fairbanks, Alaska Native Programs
University of Alaska Southeast

This publication was supported in part by grants from the Alaska
Humanities Forum and the National Endowment for the Humanities,
a federal agency, and from the Alaska Rural Systemic Intiatives.

We would also like to thank Peter Metcalfe, Sue Kraft, Nora and
Richard Dauenhauer, and Margot Waring for their efforts to bring this
publication into being.

Will The Time Ever Come?

A TLINGIT SOURCE BOOK

Copyright © 2000 Alaska Native Knowledge Network
Center for Cross-Cultural Studies
University of Alaska Fairbanks
First Printing 2000

Produced by Metcalfe Communications
Designed by Susan Kraft
Photographs by Peter Metcalfe
Printed in the USA

Elmer E. Rasmuson Library Cataloging-In-Publication Data:

Will the time ever come? : a Tlingit source book / edited by Andrew hope III and
Thomas F. Thornton. — Fairbanks, Alaska : Alaska Native Knowledge Network,
Center for Cross-Cultural Studies, University of Alaska Fairbanks; c2000.
152 p. : ill., maps ; 23 cm.

Notes: The Tlingit Tribes and Clans conference was held on May 5-10, 1993 in Haines,
Alaska.

1. Tlingit Indian — History. 2. Tlingit Indians — Social life and customs. 3. Tlingit
Indians — Intellectual life — 20th century. 4. Tlingit Indians — Bibliography. I.
Title. II. Hope, Andrew. III. Thornton, Thomas F.

E99.T6 W55 2000

ISBN 1-877962-34-1

Front Cover Artwork: "Chilkat Spirit" by Mike A. Jackson
The artwork that appears in Part III, List of Tlingit Tribes, Clans & Clan Houses is
by Mike A. Jackson.

TABLE OF CONTENTS

INTRODUCTION 6

PART I: TLINGIT HISTORY & TRADITIONS 11

    An Annotated Tlingit Bibliography, by Sergei Kan 13

    On Migrations, by Andrew Hope 23

    Inhabitants of Burning Wood Fort, by Harold Jacobs 34

    The Kiks.ádi Survival March of 1804, by Herb Hope 48

CLAN CONFERENCE PHOTOS 80

PART II: CONTEMPORARY ISSUES & PROJECTS 91

    The Sounds of English and Tlingit, by Richard Dauenhauer 93

    Building a Tlingit Resource Atlas, by Thomas F. Thornton 98

    Subsistence and Contemporary Tlingit Culture,
        by Steve J. Langdon 117

    Naming in the Year 2000, by Ellen Hope Hays 124

PART III: APPENDIX 127

    Letter from Frederica de Laguna 129

    Taanta K̲wáan, George Emmons manuscript 131

    T'aak̲u K̲wáan, George Emmons manuscript 138

    L'uknax̲.ádi, George Emmons manuscript 142

    Xát´ka.aayi, George Emmons manuscript 144

    Sik'nax̲.ádi, George Emmons manuscript 145

    List of Tlingit Tribes, Clans & Clan Houses 148

INTRODUCTION

BY ANDY HOPE

Tlingit elders tell me that our ancestors were too polite and deferential to non-Tlingits in regards to our language and traditions. Our ancestors thought that white people would think that the Tlingit were talking "behind their backs" if they spoke the Tlingit language. This deference when added to the missionaries' legacy of forced acculturation put at risk the rich heritage of our culture.

The Conference of Tlingit Tribes and Clans, more informally known as the Tlingit Clan Conference, was organized to provide a forum for traditional Tlingit knowledge. The first conference was held in Haines and Klukwan in 1993. There have been three conferences since.

The Tlingit Clan Conference is an unincorporated group of individuals (Tlingit and non-Tlingit) committed to documenting and disseminating educational materials about Tlingit knowledge. It is an appropriate forum, based on traditional Tlingit social structure, with a modern educational mission.

In December, 1995, I began work for the Alaska Rural Systemic Initiative, a partnership between the Alaska Federation of Natives, the National Science Foundation, and the University of Alaska Fairbanks. The purpose of the project is to integrate Alaska Native knowledge into the math, science and technology curricula of rural Alaska schools. The project later was expanded to include social studies and language arts curricula with funding from the Annenberg Foundation.

The Alaska Rural Systemic Initiative/Alaska Rural Challenge are funding the printing of this book to answer the question posed by Angoon elder Matthew Fred at the 1993 conference: "Will the time ever come?"

The time has come to provide more access to traditional Native knowledge. This can only improve the spiritual, mental, and physical health of our tribal communities.

For a Tlingit like myself, the starting point of understanding my culture is the clan structure. The idea of developing a list of Tlingit tribes and clans came to me in the early 1970s. Franz Boas' *Tsimshian Mythology* and Swanton's *Contributions to the Ethnology of the Haida,* which I purchased and read in the spring of 1974, provided inspiration for researching clan histories. Subsequently, I designed and published *Lingit At.oowoo,* a pamphlet of Tlingit clan crest illustrations and stories, with artwork courtesy of Henry Davis, Sr. and Robert Davis. I printed the book at the Sheldon Jackson College print shop in Sitka.

From the beginning of my publishing efforts I recognized the need for a complete book of Tlingit crests. Such a book would require a comprehensive list of Tlingit tribes, clans and clan houses. I began my first list in the summer of 1976.

Over the ensuing years, I continued gathering illustrations, source data and text for a crest manuscript (see the list of my sources in Appendix B).

In late 1977 I was contracted by the National Park Service to research the origin of the totem poles in the Sitka park. This research provided more source material for my crest manuscript. All of the poles in the park originated on Prince of Wales Island, and I had to dig out the Haida, as well as the Tlingit clans that resided in the communities at the time the poles were taken. Once I identified the clans, it was a process of matching up the respective clan crests with the figures on the poles to identify the original owners of the poles, and in turn, to document the history of each pole. The manuscript that came out of the Sitka park research was entitled *Sacred Forms.*

As I continued working on the crest manuscript, I was struck by the fact that traditional Tlingit social organization, i.e.,

Tlingit common law, provided a rock solid foundation for such contemporary manifestations of Tlingit life as subsistence and tribal government. I came to realize that the further we drifted from Tlingit traditions, the more trouble we encountered.

In 1987, Klukwan Heritage Foundation provided me with a grant that underwrote continued research for the *Sacred Forms* manuscript.

During my research, I became aware that whatever lists existed of Tlingit tribes, clans and clan houses did not belong to Tlingits — we had no ownership. Almost all of the existing lists were developed by non-Tlingits: ethnographers, anthropologists, artifact collectors, linguists, etc. One of the major obstacles to Tlingit ownership of a Tlingit list derives from the fact that, under traditional law, Tlingit clans are autonomous — there is no supreme Tlingit political authority or overall organization in place to take such action as adopting an official list. A contemporary regional organization such as Central Council of Tlingit and Haida Indian Tribes (T&H) does not have the authority to adopt such a list.

In the late 1980s, I made a series of recommendations to T&H that would have resulted in a comprehensive list. In June 1989, I recommended to the T&H Tribal Court Planning Task Force that clan/clan houses be inventoried in each community. I also recommended that guidelines be developed for recognizing clan houses, including those that no longer exist, and maintaining those that still stand. I organized the "Contemporary Native Land Use Workshop" in August 1989 that recommended T&H sponsor a tribal common law conference of elders and clan leaders. At a November 1989 workshop that preceded the Sealaska Corporation annual meeting, the foundation was laid for what became the Southeast Native Subsistence Commission. At this meeting I recommended that a conference of Tlingit and Kaigani Haida clans be held to provide clan endorsements that would strengthen the legal basis of the commission.

My recommendations to the subsistence commission were followed with a November 6, 1989 letter to Ed Warren and Joe Hotch in which I requested that the Tribal Court Planning Task

Force, which had scheduled a meeting in Klukwan for December 1989, request Sealaska Corporation, Klukwan, Inc. and other organizations to fund a conference of representatives of the respective clans of the Kaigani Haida and the Tlingit of Southeast Alaska to reaffirm the customary and traditional laws of the clans.

The idea lay dormant for two years until Ed Warren wrote a letter on behalf of Joe Hotch in December 1991 requesting my assistance in organizing a clan conference. Warren's request coincided with the start up of the Southeast Alaska Tribal Council (SEATC), a coalition of federally recognized Indian tribal governments. Formal organization of the first clan conference planning sessions took place under the auspices of SEATC and was funded by Klukwan Heritage Foundation. Planning meetings took place in Anchorage during the first BIA Tribal Service Providers conference in January 1992, Ketchikan in May 1992 during a SEATC meeting, June 1992 during another SEATC meeting, and August 1992 in Sitka at yet another SEATC meeting.

Beginning in January 1993, we conducted planning meetings by teleconference, usually every two weeks, until the month prior to the conference, when we had them once a week or more. The planning committee was the key to the eventual success of the first conference. It included representatives from Southeast Alaska, British Columbia and the Yukon. The teleconferences were underwritten by Ketchikan Indian Corporation, Klukwan Heritage Foundation and the Sitka Tribe of Alaska.

To be as inclusive as possible, I invited the Tlingit of British Columbia and Yukon. I also invited the participation of the tribes that neighbor Tlingit country: the Tsimshian of Alaska and British Columbia, the Kwakuitl of British Columbia, the Kaigani Haida and the Tagish, Tahltan and Tutchone Athapascan tribes of Canada.

The gathering that took place in May of 1993 was the closest we've ever come to a gathering of all Tlingit tribes, clans and clan houses. Such a gathering never occurred, so far as we know, in pre-contact times. Though there have been many, many large intertribal gatherings over the years, such as memorials, pole raisings, ANB conventions, and house dedications, these were never inclusive of all tribes and clans as such. The biannual *Celebrations of Tlingit, Haida and Tsimshians,* sponsored by Sealaska Heritage Foundation are certainly inclusive, but these are essentially gatherings of nations rather than tribes and clans.

Nearly 500 people signed the attendance book at our conference in Klukwan that began on May 5, 1993. The participants quickly adapted to the structure of the conference: general presentations in the morning, meetings and workshops in the afternoon, performances in the evening. Probably for the first time ever, practitioners came together with scholars as equals to discuss their mutual knowledge of and experience with the cultures indigenous to this part of the world.

The following pages include papers that were presented at the first conference and other papers, now completed, that at the time were works in progress. Also included in the text are several previously unpublished manuscripts by Lt. George Emmons, a noted amateur ethnographer who worked among the Tlingits in the late nineteenth century. In the appendix, you will find the list of Tlingit Tribes and Clans that I've developed over the years, a work still in progress.

I readily acknowledge we can expect no unanimity of opinion when it comes to discussions of Tlingit clans and tribes. Too much has been lost and too little was accurately recorded. But if this book stimulates discussion and more research then it has been worth the effort.

Juneau, Alaska
April, 1999

PART I

TLINGIT HISTORY & TRADITIONS

AN ANNOTATED TLINGIT BIBLIOGRAPHY

BY SERGEI KAN
DEPARTMENT OF ANTHROPOLOGY/
NATIVE AMERICAN STUDIES PROGRAM
DARTMOUTH COLLEGE

Sergei Kan is an anthropologist who was born and raised in the Soviet Union before moving to the United States. Currently an Associate Professor of Anthropology at Dartmouth College, Kan has written many scholarly articles on Tlingit culture and ethnohistory and a book (see Kan 1989) on the nineteenth century Tlingit memorial feast ritual, or potlatch as anthropologists call it. His command of the Russian source material on the Tlingit is unparalleled, and he has brought much of it to bear on his studies of Tlingit ethnohistory. In his remarks, Professor Kan stressed the need for Natives to engage in their own historical work. The annotated bibliography he presents here provides a very useful starting point into the written works for any researcher, as it not only lists key sources of information but also critically evaluates and links the materials in constructive ways.

The following is a brief summary of my presentation to the Clan Conference on the topic of compiling an annotated comprehensive bibliography of the existing sources on Tlingit culture and history.*

Since 1978 I have been engaged in anthropological research in which I have tried to combine the use of a variety of published and unpublished written sources with the information I myself obtained from knowledgeable elders and tradition-bearers in Sitka, Angoon and a number of other Tlingit communities. In con-

*This essay was written in 1993-1994 and updated in 1999 with kind assistance from Thomas F. Thornton.

trast to my anthropological predecessors, I have paid particular attention to the valuable information on the nineteenth century Tlingit economic, social, and religious life contained in Russian-language sources.

Over the years I have accumulated numerous reprints and copies of archival materials, early travellers' accounts, and published scholarly articles from well-known as well as obscure journals in several European languages. I believe the time has come to put together a bibliography containing all of these major sources on Tlingit history and culture that would be of use to the Tlingit people themselves as well as the non-Tlingit scholars and the general public. While an annotated bibliography of the literature on Native Americans of the Northwest Coast does exist (Robert S. Grumet Native Americans of the Northwest Coast; Indiana University Press; 1979), a Tlingit bibliography does not. There is an unpublished, briefly annotated bibliography of the works on the Tlingit and Haida from 1741 to 1867 produced by Robert E. Price in 1990 and updated in 1995, but it is somewhat incomplete and slightly idiosyncratic. Russian-language sources, especially archival ones, are not given justice in it.

The bibliography I would like to put together will consist of both published and unpublished works and would cover the entire Tlingit history from the earliest European accounts of the culture to the present. The annotation will assist the reader in selecting needed materials and becoming aware of the authors' sources of information as well as biases. I believe that an anthropologist, like myself, who works not only in the library and the archive but "in the field" (i.e., with real people) is in a better position to evaluate the strengths and the weaknesses of a particular work.

This is precisely the kind of research I did when I translated from Russian into English and prepared for publication a book entitled Tlingit Indians of Alaska (University of Alaska Press; 1985) by Fr. Anatolii Kamenskii, a Russian Orthodox missionary stationed in Sitka for several of years in the late 1890s. Kamenskii founded the St. Michael Brotherhood in Sitka in 1896, toured southeastern Alaska as the head priest of that area, ad-

ministered medicine to Indian people, and collected ethnographic data. He did not speak Tlingit but probably under
stood it and had developed rather close relationships with his
Tlingit parishioners. He was not, however, as tolerant of and
sympathetic towards the Native culture as some of the other
Russian Orthodox workers; in fact, his attitudes were closer to
those of most of the leading Presbyterian missionaries of the
time. In order to separate fact from fiction and speculation in
Kamenskii's account of the past and present life and world view
of the Tlingit, I had to establish his educational and ideological
background, attitudes toward the Tlingit, familiarity with the
previous Russian and American works on the subject or the
lack thereof, as well as to trace his major activities in Sitka and
the surrounding communities in his role as a missionary priest.
As a result of this detailed research, I concluded that despite
numerous errors and some strong anti-Native (as well as anti-
American) biases, Fr. Kamenskii did report several important
historical facts and some valuable bits of cultural data that cannot be found in the works of his Russian or American contem-
poraries, whether they were missionaries, government officials,
or anthropologists.

In a similar fashion I plan to evaluate the work of all of the
major professional anthropologists who wrote about the Tlingit, from Krause to de Laguna. Special attention will be paid to
two recently published works both of which are major contributions to the literature on the topic. One of them is George
Emmons' lengthy manuscript The Tlingit Indians (1991), pains-
takingly edited by Frederica de Laguna, which covers a variety
of topics from technology and economy to social organization
and traditional religion. The other is only known to a small
group of scholars of Alaska history and ethnology who read
Russian. It is the work of a Russian scholar, Andrei V. Grinev,
published in Novosibirsk (Russia) in 1991, entitled Tlingit Indians During the Era of Russian America (1741-1867). This is
the first substantial work on the history of Tlingit-Russian relations which utilizes a variety of key sources from several Russian archives. Its additional strength is in the author's interest

in the Native side of the Russian-Tlingit encounter. Being an anthropologist by training, Grinev tries not simply to document this history but to evaluate the effects of the Russian presence in southeastern Alaska on Tlingit economy, technology, social organization, religion, warfare, and language. While we might take issue with some of his conclusions, the book clearly merits translation into English and publication in our country. In addition to scholarly publications, I would like to include in this bibliography difficult-to-find and obscure works that do add to our understanding of Tlingit history and culture. Thus, for example, in my own research on the history and cultural significance of Tlingit Christianity, I have gleaned some interesting information from such rarely-cited works as Charles Replogle's 1904 book <u>Among the Indians of Alaska</u> (which deals with the work of the Quakers in Juneau in the early 1900s) and Alfred Gilliard's brief biography of Charles Newton (entitled <u>Gentle Eagle</u>), a prominent Salvation Army leader in Kake, published by the Salvation Army in London in 1955.

The section of my bibliography covering archival materials should be of special interest to the Tlingit audience. Among other things, it would include information on the unpublished fieldnotes of some prominent anthropologists who worked in Tlingit country and whose published studies are well-known but are often less detailed than their archival collections. Thus few people are aware of Ronald Olson's unpublished field notes located in the Bancroft Library of the University of California, Berkeley, which contain the data that served as the basis of his well-known 1967 monograph on Tlingit social structure and social life.

A major part of my bibliography will also be devoted to describing and appraising the documents contained in the archives of the Russian Orthodox Church, particularly the so-called Alaska Orthodox Church Collection (Manuscript Division, Library of Congress; available on microfilm from the Alaska State Library, Juneau). Over the years I have utilized this valuable source of information to research and write about such important aspects of Tlingit life in the nineteenth-early twentieth century as the role of Orthodox brotherhoods in Tlingit religious and social life around the turn of the century, Russian missionaries' attitudes towards and attempts to change Tlingit memorial rites, and the relations between the Russian, "Creole" and Anglo-American populations in Sitka and Juneau, and the Tlingit Orthodox parish members. While many important documents from this collection have already been used, this and several other collections (e.g., the M.Z. Vinokouroff Collection in the Alaska State Library) remain a rich but largely untapped source of information on the religious and secular life of several Tlingit communities (e.g., they contain information on marriage practices, inheritance, interclan relations, economic life, the role of women in social life, celebration of religious holidays by Tlingit communities, competition between the various missions that worked among the Tlingit, etc.).

I concluded my presentation at the Clan Conference with an appeal to the members of the audience to engage in their own historical work. While written sources discussed here are valuable, they often reflect the observers' own research agenda and not what the Tlingit community itself would have liked to preserve as a record of its history and culture. Thus I would like to suggest that we need to know more about individual Tlingit leaders of the past, whether they were men or women, church wardens ("starostas") or sisterhood presidents, political activists or prominent storytellers and teachers. Relatives and descendants of such men and women are in a better position to collect this kind of information than scholars residing outside Alaska. (For an excellent example of this type of pioneering work see the Dauenhauers' 1994 collection.) I also urged those participants in the conference who are interested in documenting and preserving their own history and culture to collect and duplicate old family photographs, non-traditional ceremonial regalia (e.g., church brotherhood sashes), tape and video recordings of memorials and other Native events and to share them with researchers, whenever this seems to be appropriate. I then pointed out that in return, we, historians and anthropologists, should try our best to reciprocate by sharing information on the family and community history that we happen to come across in our library and archival research. Thus, while examining the M. Z. Vinokouroff Collection at the Alaska State Library, I recently came accross a series of letters exchanged in the 1960s-1970s between Mr. Vinokouroff (who worked at the Library of Congress and whose grandfather served as a priest in Sitka during the Russian-American Company era) and protodeacon Innocent Williams of Sitka's St. Michael Cathedral. In addition, our own photographs and recordings made in "the field" have already become historical documents in their own right. Thus, I now have such interesting recordings as the one I made in 1980 of the late William Nelson's account of the life of his close clan relative, Eli Katanook, or the history of the Orthodox churches in Killisnoo and Angoon that I recorded from the late Jimmy George, Sr. in December of 1979.

There is a lot of room for cooperation between professional scholars and Native historians here. This Clan Conference might very well become an excellent beginning in an important project of compiling a detailed, diverse, and reliable record of Tlingit history and culture for generations to come.

In conclusion I would like to offer my own list of major published sources on Tlingit culture and history with some brief comments. I have tried to select publications which might be of special interest to Tlingit readers:

1. Books:

- Dauenhauer, Nora Marks and Richard Dauenhauer, eds. (1987) Haa Shuká, Our Ancestors: Tlingit Oral Narratives. Seattle: University of Washington Press.

  [A carefully annotated collection of Tlingit narratives compiled by the Dauenhauers from well-known Tlingit story-tellers during the last twenty-five years and presented in Tlingit and English—the best anthology of Tlingit folklore ever published].

- Dauenhauer, Nora Marks and Richard Dauenhauer, eds. (1990) Haa Tuwunáagu Yis, for Healing Our Spirit. Seattle: University of Washington Press.

  [A bilingual publication of some of the best examples of Tlingit oratory recorded between 1899 and 1988 and carefully annotated by the editors; a detailed introduction explaining key aspects of Tlingit social and ceremonial culture as well as brief biographies of master orators add to the book's value].

- Dauenhauer, Nora Marks and Richard Dauenhauer, eds. (1994) Haa Kusteeyí, Our Culture: Tlingit Life Stories. Seattle: University of Washington Press.

  [The book features biographies and life histories of more than fifty men and women, most of them born between 1880 and 1910. It is not only the first collection which combines interesting accounts gathered from living memory of Tlingit elders with historical documents and photographs, but is also a well-written introduction to the last one hundred years of Tlingit social and political history].

- Emmons, George T. (1991) The Tlingit Indians. Edited with additions by Frederica de Laguna. Seattle: University of Washington Press.

[A comprehensive and detailed description of nineteenth-century Tlingit culture by Lt. Emmons who spent a great deal of time in southeastern Alaska in the 1880s-1900s; Emmons was sympathetic to the Tlingit people, spoke some Tlingit or at least understood it well, and had good rapport with many prominent Native leaders and elders].

- Goldschmidt, Walter and Theodore Haas. 1946. "Possessory Rights of the Natives of Southeastern Alaska." Unpublished report. Washington D.C.: Commissioner of Indian Affairs.

[Note: this report was edited and expanded, and published in 1998, under the title Haa Aaní, Our Land: Tlingit and Haida Land Rights and Use. Sealaska Heritage Foundation and University of Washington Press.]

- Kamenskii, Anatolii (1985) Tlingit Indians of Alaska. Translated, introduced, and supplemented by Sergei Kan. Fairbanks: University of Alaska Press.
  [see discussion above].

- Kan, Sergei (1989) Symbolic Immortality: Tlingit Potlatch of the Nineteenth Century. Washington, D.C.: Smithsonian Institution Press.

[A detailed reconstruction and analysis of the most important Tlingit ceremony and related aspects of Tlingit culture, based on the author's own field research in Alaska conducted in 1979-1987 as well as numerous published and archival sources].

- Kan, Sergei (1999) Memory Eternal: Tlingit Culture and Russian Orthodox Christianity Through Two Centuries. Seattle: University of Washington Press.

[The book, based on almost twenty years of fieldwork and archival research experience in Southeast Alaska, combines anthropology and history, anecdote and interpretation to portray an encounter between the Tlingit people and the Russian Orthodox Church in the late 1700s and analyze the native Orthodoxy that developed over the next two hundred years. It also contains mini-biographies of many active Orthodox parish members and church workers who combined a commitment to Orthodoxy with an adherence to traditional Tlingit beliefs and memorial ceremonies].

- Krause, Aurel (1956 [1885]) The Tlingit Indians. Seattle: University of Washington Press.

[Despite some of its errors, this work remains one of the major accounts of the nineteenth-century Tlingit culture based on a six-month stay in southeastern Alaska, particularly in the Haines-Klukwan area].

- Krause, Aurel and Arthur Krause (1993 [1881-82]). To the Chukchi Peninsula and to the Tlingit Indians 1881-82. Journals and Letters of Aurel and Arthur Krause. Translated by Margot Krause McCaffrey. Fairbanks: University of Alaska Press.

[A good supplement to Krauses's book, these previously unpublished documents give the reader a better sense of the Krause brothers' relationships with their Tlingit hosts and their experience in Chilkat country].

- de Laguna, Frederica (1960) The Story of a Tlingit Community. Bureau of American Ethnology Bulletin 172. Washington, D.C.: U.S. Government Printing Office.

[An important study of the history of Angoon, based on archeological and archival materials as well as oral testimony collected in the summers of 1949 and 1950].

- de Laguna, Frederica (1972) Under Mount Saint Elias: The History and Culture of the Yakutat Tlingit. Smithsonian Contributions to Anthropology 7. Washington: Smithsonian Institution Press.

  [This is a three-volume treasure of information on Tlingit culture and history; despite its focus on Yakutat, much of the data applies to the Tlingit culture in general. While written sources were used, the bulk of the data was collected from Tlingit elders during several stays in Yakutat between 1949 and 1954].

- Elizabeth Nyman and Jeff Leer (1993) Gágiwdul.àt {with barred l}: Brought Forth to Reconfirm: the Legacy of a Taku River Tlingit Clan. Yukon Native Language Center and Alaska Native Language Center.

  [Told by Mrs. Nyman in her native Tlingit language in the 1980s and translated and edited by Leer, these six narratives movingly relate ancient legends and traditional stories about the Yanyeidí clan people of the Taku River region].

- Oberg, Kalervo (1971 [1937]) The Social Economy of the Tlingit Indians.

  [Despite some errors and a certain superficiality, this work contains some valuable information on Tlingit economy and social organization which was collected by the author during his stay in Klukwan in the winter of 1931-32 and his visits to several other Tlingit communities].

- Olson, Ronald L. (1967) Social Structure and Social Life of the Tlingit Indians in Alaska. University of California Anthropological Records 26.

  [Despite publishing some gossip and other sensitive information which should not have appeared in print, Olson offers a great deal of valuable information on the history of Tlingit ꞩwáans, clans and houses as well as on the culture in general, which he collected from a number of Tlingit friends and informants in the 1930s, 40s, and 50s].

- Peck, Cyrus E., Sr. (1975) The Tides People. Juneau: Indian Studies Program.

  [An interesting collection of legends and other information on Tlingit history and culture by a well-known Native historian].

- Swanton, John R. (1909) Tlingit Myths and Texts. Bureau of American Ethnology Bulletin 39. Washington, D.C.: U.S. Government Printing Office.

  [While not as reliable as the the the work of the Dauenhauers, this is a rich collection of Tlingit folklore collected in Sitka and Wrangell in the winter and spring of 1904].

2. Essays and Articles:

- Billman, Esther (1964) A Potlatch Feast in Sitka, Alaska. Anthropological Papers of the University of Alaska 14(2):55-64.

  [The real author of this fascinating eyewitness account of a 1877 L'uknax̱.ádi memorial feast is William Wells who recorded it in English in the mid-1880s while attending the Sitka Training School].

- Garfield, Viola (1947) Historical Aspects of Tlingit Clans in Angoon, Alaska. American Anthropologist 49 (3): 438-452.

  [Some valuable information on Angoon social history and social structure collected by a prominent Northwest Coast anthropologist during a relatively brief stay in Angoon in 1945].

- Henrikson, Steve (1993) "Terrifying Visages" : War Helmets of the Tlingit Indians. American Indian Art Magazine Winter 1993: 48-59.

[A clearly written and nicely illustrated overview and reinterpretation of the artistic symbolism, meaning and function (military and ceremonial) of the Tlingit war helmet, based on the author's thorough knowledge of the relevant museum artifacts and conversations with Tlingit elders].

- Jacobs, Mark, Jr. and Mark Jacobs, Sr. (1982) Southeast Alaska Native Foods. Pp. 112-130 In Raven's Bones, ed. by Andrew Hope, III. Sitka: Sitka Community Association.

[The first publication on Tlingit food by a prominent Tlingit historian who used personal experience as well as the information provided by his older relatives].

- Kan, Sergei (1985) Russian Orthodox Brotherhoods among the Tlingit: Missionary Goals and Native Response. Ethnohistory 32 (3): 196-223.

[A study of an important but previously ignored aspect of Tlingit social and religious life in the first half of the twentieth century, based on archival research and interviews with elders].

- Kan, Sergei (1987) Memory Eternal: Russian Orthodoxy and the Tlingit Mortuary Complex. Arctic Anthropology 24 (1): 32-55.

[A study of the effects of Orthodox Christianity on the Tlingit funerals and memorial rites, including the "forty-day party," based on archival research, interviews with elders, and personal observations recorded in 1979-1984].

- de Laguna, Frederica (1990) Tlingit. Pp. 203-228 In Handbook of North American Indians, vol. 7 (Northwest Coast). Ed. by W. Suttles. Washington, D.C.: Smithsonian Institution Press.

[A comprehensive sketch of Tlingit culture by its foremost scholar who has been studying the subject for almost fifty years].

- Moss, Madonna L. (1993) Shellfish, Gender, and Status on the Northwest Coast: Reconciling Archeological, Ethnographic, and Ethnohistorical Records of the Tlingit. American Anthropologist 95 (3): 631-52.

[The best example of the "new anthropology" of Tlingit culture which combines extensive archeological data with the use of previously published sources and interview data, much of it collected by the author herself in the Angoon area in the last fifteen years].

- Oberg, Kalervo (1934) Crime and Punishment in Tlingit Society. American Anthropologist 36:145-156.

[The first attempt to analyze a complex system of the traditional Tlingit criminal law].

- Price, Robert E. (1995) "Bibliography of Literature on Alaska History from 1741 to 1867. Alaska-Siberia Research Center Publication #7. Juneau.

- Shotridge, Louis (1928) The Emblems of Tlingit Culture. The Museum Journal 19:350-377.

[An interesting description of the history of some of the greatest Tlingit at.óow (clan regalia) by a prominent and controversial Tlingit collector and Native historian].

- Swanton, John R. (1908) Social Conditions, Beliefs, and Linguistic Relationship of the Tlingit Indians. Pp. 391-512 In 26th Annual Report of the Bureau of American Ethnology for the Years 1904-05. Washington, D.C.: U.S. Government Printing Office.

22   Will the Time Ever Come?

[Despite its limitations, this is an important study of Tlingit culture, the first one carried out by a professionally-trained anthropologist who interviewed a number of knowledgeable Tlingit in Sitka and Wrangell during his three-month stay there in 1904].

- Thornton, Thomas F. (1997) Know Your Place: the Organization of Tlingit Geographic Knowledge. Ethnology 36(4): 295-307.

[Using the place-name inventory of a 83-year-old Tlingit elder and drawing on his own long-standing research on Tlingit geographic knowledge, Thornton effectively analyzes how geographic names form an essential part of Tlingit social being and integrate physical, sociological, and spiritual landscapes in practical ways].

- Veniaminov, Ivan [Bishop Innokentii; St. Innocent] (1984 [1840]) Notes on the Koloshi [Tlingit]. Pp. 380-451 In Veniaminov's Notes on the Islands of the Unalashka District. Translated by L. T. Black and R.H.Geoghegan. Fairbanks: University of Alaska Press.

[The earliest attempt to offer a sympathetic and fairly detailed description of Tlingit culture in the first decades of the nineteenth century by Alaska's best-known Russian Orthodox missionary who spent several years in Sitka in the 1830s, not only studying Tlingit language and culture but preaching the word of God and administering vaccination against small-pox].

- Worl, Rosita and Charles Smythe (1986) Jennie Thlunaut: Master Chilkat Blanket Artist. Pp. 127-146 In The Artist Behind the Work. Fairbanks: University of Alaska Museum.

[A sensitive biography of one of the best traditional master Chilkat blanket artists, written by two anthropologists one of whom is closely related to Mrs. Thlunaut].

ON MIGRATIONS

BY ANDREW HOPE

The history of the Tlingit is woven in the clans, the central units of the social structure. A good historian by Tlingit standards is someone who knows the history of his clan, its origins, development, subdivisions, settlements, migrations, and material and symbolic property. These are long stories, traditionally told over many nights around winter fires and authenticated in ceremonies by knowledgeable listeners. Ideally, Tlingits interested in learning more about their identities should develop a historical consciousness of both their mother's and father's clans and those of their grandparents as well. But where does one begin? By tracing the migrations of his own clan, Tlingit historian Andy Hope in this paper offers one model for how a Tlingit person interested in discovering more about his or her shagóon (heritage and identity) might proceed.

I was born in Sitka, Alaska, an ancient Tlingit community on the outer coast of Baranof Island in Central Southeast Alaska. Sitka is derived from the Tlingit Sheey.at'iká, "the outer edge of a branch pointing downward, with knotholes running through," a poetic description of the area's topography. Sitka is the homeland of my father's clan, the Kiks.ádi of the Raven moiety. The Tlingit clans are divided into two equal sides or moieties. The Tlingit follow the line of the mother. My mother's homeland is Wrangell. The Tlingit name for Wrangell is Stax'heen, "the manner in which a person grits his teeth after drinking water from the glacial lakes." I am a descendant of X'aan Hít, Red Clay house, of the Sik'naxádi, "Grindstone people," clan of the Wolf moiety. My Tlingit name is X'ustanch, "Killer Whales Coming Down in a Wave, Going to War."

24   Will the Time Ever Come?

The Sik'na<u>x</u>.ádi ancestors came to the coast from the interior plains of Alaska. The time that this migration occurred is unknown. The route the migrating party took is also unknown, although it seems likely that they traveled along the coast between the Cordova area at the mouth of the Copper River and the Yakutat area. The distance from the Copper River Delta to the Antlein River is approximately 200 miles. This region of the northern gulf coast of Alaska features Mt. Logan and Mt. St. Elias (the second and third highest peaks on the North American continent), the Bagley Ice Field, and the Bering and Malaspina Glaciers. The migration traditions of the Kwáashk'i <u>K</u>wáan, a Raven moiety clan that still resides in the Yakutat area, reflect two migrations, one on the waters of the gulf coast and one over the glaciers and ice fields of this region of the Alaskan gulf coast.

> One of them came down the Copper River and settled near the mouth, another came along the ocean in a big skin boat, bringing his family of course as they all did.
>
> But her family's brother's ancestor came across the ice, glaciers, till they saw land, till they saw good land, which was here at Yakutat. Those that came along the ocean got here first, the glacier migrants arrived here later.
>
> The migrators over the glaciers maybe consumed a hundred years in migrating to Yakutat. When they reached here, the Indians who had come along the coast were already at Yakutat. When the ocean travelers arrived here, there was <u>no one</u> living here...
>
> *(Maggie Harry, in deLaguna 1972)*

Upon reaching the Yakutat area they settled on the Ahrnklin River, At.aaní Tlein, "Big town of Animals" in Tlingit. This community was located about two miles above the mouth and between branches of the Ahrnklin. According to John Swanton (1908), this community was founded by Kichihdaalx', "Heavy Wings," a prominent figure in Tlingit mythology.

When did people originally come to this region? Archeological research and fieldwork did not begin in Southeast Alaska until the late forties. The latest available archeological findings are as follows:

It is impossible to categorically assert how long the Tlingit people have occupied Southeast Alaska since artifacts do not speak a language. Linguistic evidence of a highly qualified nature presented by Michael Krauss suggests the Tlingit language grew out of the organic amalgamation of a number of languages and dialects which had separated individually from a Proto-Athabascan ancestral language some 4-6,000 years ago.

There are presently four possibilities concerning Tlingit occupation of Southeast Alaska with two generally given greater likelihood than the other two. The first (weak) suggests they could have been the earliest occupants of the region (some 10,000 years ago) and later developed new tools; few archaeologists would assert this. Secondly (strongest), they could have entered 3,500 years ago and continuously developed since that time. The tool types in use 3,500 years ago (ground slate points, adzes, bone points and harpoon heads), were still utilized to some extent by the Tlingit and Haida with whom first contact was made in the 18th century. Davis (1991) has recently made a third suggestion (strong), based on the appearance of forts and changes in ground slate tool types, that the ancestral Tlingit appeared in the region about 1,500 years ago. Finally (weak), the specificity of Tlingit oral traditions of migration into the region from the south along the coast and from the interior down the river valleys could be interpreted as movement into the region only in the last 500-1,000 years.

(Langdon 1991)

The migrating party eventually sold the Ahrnklin land to the Teiḵweidí, another wolf moiety clan. The Teiḵweidí have clan houses in Saxman, Angoon, and Yakutat.

The young people began to go for a walk and made a long trip. They found some people at Arhnklin. The name of the river is Aantlein, short for 'big town of animals.' The young people fell in love with the mountains and the river. They went back and told

26 Will the Time Ever Come?

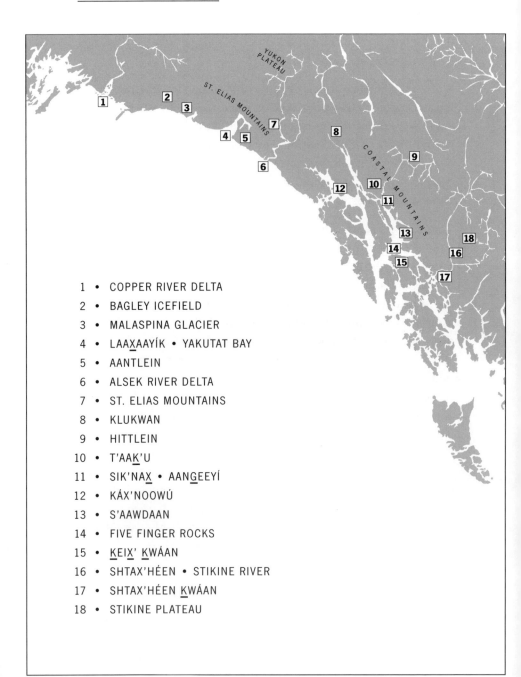

1 • COPPER RIVER DELTA
2 • BAGLEY ICEFIELD
3 • MALASPINA GLACIER
4 • LAAXAAYÍK • YAKUTAT BAY
5 • AANTLEIN
6 • ALSEK RIVER DELTA
7 • ST. ELIAS MOUNTAINS
8 • KLUKWAN
9 • HITTLEIN
10 • T'AAK'U
11 • SIK'NAX • AANGEEYÍ
12 • KÁX'NOOWÚ
13 • S'AAWDAAN
14 • FIVE FINGER ROCKS
15 • KEIX' KWÁAN
16 • SHTAX'HÉEN • STIKINE RIVER
17 • SHTAX'HÉEN KWÁAN
18 • STIKINE PLATEAU

their chief how pretty that river is. The Chief's name was Gutleniyu;
he was the chief of the Gaaw Hít (Drum House).

So the chief went to meet the other chief, the chief of the Yanyeidí
who owned the land, and they began to talk about it. So Gutleniyu
bought the Aantlein land for a big copper, tinaa. The copper was as
long as from the tips of his fingers to his chin, when his head was
bent back, and was worth 10 slaves. Then all the Gaaw Híttaan came
up there and the Yanyeidí moved to Southeastern Alaska, to Taku,
where some of them live today."

(Olaf Abraham, in deLaguna 1972)

Alsek is derived from the Tlingit Aalseix̱', "Back toward the
mountains." The ancestors moved northeast toward the Yukon
plateau and then Southeast through the Teslin plateau to the
Stikine plateau. My late uncle referred to this route as a highway. It may have been a highway, but only in a metaphorical
sense. In moving toward the Yukon plateau, the moving party
had to traverse ice fields, glaciers, while moving through the
St. Elias mountain range.

...after the original owners had sold the Aantlein land to the
Teikweidí they walked into the interior over one of the glaciers
from Russell Fiord, probably Nunatak Glacier. They went to
Shaanyuk̲a, probably on the headwaters of the Alsek, near Scotty
Creek and below Wes'katahéen (Dalton Post). It took them three
months walking. From there they went on one and a half months to
'Taku Lake,' identified as the Taku Arm of Lake Atlin...

(Maggie Harry, in deLaguna 1972)

Louis Shotridge documented the conditions of this route in
"Ghost of Courageous Adventurer," an account of a Tlingit ex-
plorer who led an exploration party from Klukwan on the
Chilkat River to the Copper River delta, virtually the same route
traveled by the Sik'nax̱.ádi party, albeit in the opposite direction.

Chilkat is not the original home of the (Shangukeidí) Tlingit Indians; they immigrated to this region from the south, and like any

immigrants who have found themselves in strange country, when they came to settle at the head of Lynn Canal, they did not know that the adjacent regions were inhabited. Their inland hunting grounds, for some years, were confined to the neighboring mountains, but the interior of the country was shut off by ice, that is by glaciers which filled the canyon passages at the head for the Chilkat River. The geographical knowledge of the people who were found inhabiting the Chilkat region when the Tlingit arrived, did not cover more than a narrow strip of land toward the northern interior. Being more aggressive and virile in nature, the Tlingit immigrants did not stop to be contented with the limited area that surrounded them. Efforts were made in the way of expeditions, to become more familiar with the new country, but nothing new or important was discovered until a small party of men, under the leadership of a Shangukeidí man by the name of Gaay Shaayí (Eagle Head), ventured over what is now known as the St. Elias Range. There is no accurate geographical information to be offered to indicate the exact location of the regions referred to in the account of the journey, and we can only guess at localities by computing the time it took to walk from the starting point. The legend shows that after crossing the desert of ice, the party went along the Pacific coast all the way to what is known as Copper River. This journey on foot, which is said to have taken all of the favorable season, proved a very difficult one. Even at the present time with maps and modern equipment, one is often puzzled as to a safe course over the deserts of ice along the way.

When the explorers returned to Klukwan, the native town on the Chilkat River where I was born, only very few of the men survived to receive the honors of discovery and the prospect of acquiring riches. Some lost their lives while crossing the ice and others died of starvation. The survivors on their return told their story and made known the inhabited regions of the west coast. They also brought back iron and ivory, articles previously unknown to the Tlingit people.

(Louis Shotridge 1920)

After moving through the St. Elias range, the migrating party headed through the Yukon and Teslin plateaus of Southern Yukon Territory and Northwest British Columbia. This is a region of hundreds of lakes, some as much as 75 miles in length. The distance from Ahrnklin River to Telegraph Creek on the upper Stikine River is approximately 350 miles. Upon reaching the Stikine plateau, they encountered the Tahltan, an Athabascan tribe that still inhabits the area. The Tahltan turned the Sik'nax̱.ádi party back. The migrating party turned to the Taku River. They would have faced virtually the same conditions that they encountered when coming inland. Taku is derived from the Tlingit T'aak̲u: "the place where geese lie down" or "goose flood." To put the movement of Southeast Alaska's glaciers in perspective, in the mid-17th century the Taku Glacier abutted Taku Point and dammed the Taku River. This ice dam created a lake more than 200 feet deep that extended for tens of mile up the Taku River valley. In less than a half century the Taku Glacier receded more than 6 miles from Taku Point. The glacier now terminates 1 mile from Taku Point and may dam the river again in 100 years according to current estimates. In the Glacier Bay area, some glaciers have receded as much as 90 miles since the early 18th century.

The party moved down the Taku until they came to a place where a glacier blocked passage. They didn't know what to do. Two old women, Aawastei and Shoowteen told the party to put them in a canoe and they would travel through the ice tunnel beneath the glacier. They composed a song as they moved under the glacier. A party of young men traveled over the top of the glacier simultaneously. The women and the young men met on the coast side of the glacier. They built a fire and sent smoke signals to the people waiting on the mainland side of the glacier that they could move through the ice tunnel safely.

The migrating party continued down the Taku until they reached a place surrounded by sedimentary rock formations. They settled at this place for a time. Wolf moiety tradition refers to a Hít Tlein, "Great House," located on the Taku.

The Inklin River and the point of land at its confluence with the Taku (Nakina) is referred to as Héen Tlein (Great Water) in Tlingit. It is usually marked 'Inklin' on recent maps. Below Inklin just above the canyon on the Taku is known as Xakw'shukwa (Gravel Bar) in Tlingit. This is said to have been the original home of all the Yanyeidí and the site of the first Hít Tlein...

(McClellan 1975)

A number of Wolf moiety clans were affiliated with Hít Tlein, among them the Yanyeidí (who settled in the Canadian interior and the Juneau area)*, the Wooshkeetaan (who settled in Juneau, Angoon, Hoonah and Sitka), the Naanyaa.aayí (who settled in the Wrangell area) and the Sik'nax.ádi. According to the late Tlingit orator Suzie James, the Kaagwaantaan, Wooshkeetaan and Chookaneidí were all house groups from the same clan that divided after the Glacier Bay village was destroyed by an advancing glacier said to have been called forth by the young woman Kaasteen, an incident documented in <u>Haa Shuká</u> (1987).

One wonders what type of canoes the party used for their trip down the Taku. Did they use the cottonwood canoes Shotridge refers to in "Ghost of Courageous Adventurer?" Did they use birch bark canoes? Did they sew moose or caribou hides to make skin boats? The migrating party built three canoes near the mouth of the Taku. Perhaps they acquired the technology for building ocean going canoes when they were settled at Aantlein. Perhaps they acquired this technology after they settled at the mouth of the Taku.

...the Inland Tlingit know of Siknaxsáank'i as the coastal Taku town to which some of the upper Taku River Yanyeidi moved after the quarrel at Gravel Bar. The village is obviously Emmon's 'Sicknahsongae (Ground Stone Bay) at the head of Taku Harbor, which he says was the very first place anywhere at all to have had members of the Wolf moiety.

(McClellan 1975)

---

* For more on the history of the Taku River and the Yanyeidí clan see Nyman and Leer (1993).

There was another village just north of the Taku cannery (at Taku Inlet) which was called Siknax̱sáank'i. There were about two tribal houses at that place. The village was there long before the cannery was put there. Limestone Inlet has a humpy stream. There were no villages there. We used to get stones there for sharpening tools.

(Alexander Stevens, in Goldschmidt and Haas 1946)

From their settlement at the mouth of the Taku, the migrating party headed south through Stevens Passage. Their first stop was approximately 40 miles south of Taku Inlet at Holkam Bay. The people in one of the canoes needed water. They went ashore. The others tied their canoes to kelp beds and rested for the night. The next morning the people who had gone ashore for water had not returned. The other canoes went ashore and found the people of the thirsty canoe camped on the beach. The thirsty ones had decided to settle at this place, which they named S'awdaan: "Dungeness Crab Town."

The two remaining canoes continued southward until they reached Five Finger Rocks, about 60 miles south of Taku Inlet. One of the canoes headed west. (It should be noted here that Emmons lists the Kaagwaantaan as originating south from the Nass River as part of the Shangukeidí group. See the attached list of Tlingit Wolf moiety clan groupings. I think that Emmons is accurate in this respect; nevertheless, I offer the following account as told by my uncle.)

They traveled around the southern tip of Admiralty Island, up Chatham Strait and settled at a place they named Kax'noowú, "Grouse Fort," a canoe journey of 130 miles from Five Finger Rocks.

The Grouse Fort people lived in one house. They gathered wood daily. One group always collected more wood than the other. They argued about this. One group challenged the other to a wood gathering contest. The ones that gathered the most wood would be the supreme group. One group had been stockpiling wood secretly, an Indian way of teasing. The group that had been stockpiling wood won the contest easily. The losing group started fighting. While they were fighting, embers were kicked into woven cedar bark curtains in the house. The curtains caught fire and burned the house timbers. The wolf moiety clan name Kawagaanihittaan, "Burnt Timber House People," came from this incident. The clan name was later contracted to Kaagwaantaan.

The Kaagwaantaan are one of the largest Tlingit clans today.

> The last canoe moved on to Kake, 100 miles south of Taku Inlet. Kake is derived from the Tlingit Keix': 'the noise a person makes when walking on gravel.' (Another interpretation is that the name is a contraction of a Tlingit phrase meaning 'The Town that Never Sleeps.') Some of the party settled at a river named Was'heení, 'Louse Creek.' The migrating party continued on to Wrangell, 150 miles Southeast of Taku Inlet. They were greeted by the Kiks.ádi, a Raven moiety clan. The Kiks.ádi asked the travelers where they had come from. The travelers replied that they had moved down the Taku and had settled for a time at Taku Harbor. The Kiks.ádi replied that they gathered grinding stones in that area and gave the travelers the name Sik'nax.ádi, 'Grindstone People.' The Kiks.ádi had preceded the Sik'nax.ádi to Shtax'héen. They had migrated from the Naas River area to the south. The Kiks.ádi established clan houses in Saxman, Wrangell and Sitka.

> ...a name once given (to a clan house), survive(s) the mere structure.

> *(George Emmons 1916)*

The Naanyaa.aayí arrived in the Shtax'héen shortly after the Sik'nax.ádi. Naanyaa.aayí is derived from the Tlingit Naa, "upriver" and niyaa, "direction." These two clans are closely related, claiming the same crests. A number of the crests that these clans claim came from the Tsimshians following warfare. The ownership of the Naanyaa.aayí Killer Whale crest was obtained in this manner. The clan houses of the Naanyaa.aayí and the Sik'nax.ádi are as follows:

NAANYAA.AAYÍ
X'atgu Hít-Blue Shark House
Hít Tlein-Great House
X'atgu Naasi Hít- Shark's Intestines House
Kook Hít- Box House
Aan Shooka Hít- House at the far end of Wrangell Village

SIK'NAX.ÁDI
X'aan Hít- Red Clay House
Aank' Hít- Cane House

The Kaagwaantaan of Sitka also claim Kook Hít as a clan house. As previously mentioned, Hít Tlein was an important settlement during the migration down the Taku. The Naanyaa.aayí are the only Tlingit clan to claim the name Hít Tlein for a clan house.

X̲OODZIDAA̲ K̲WÁAN

Inhabitants of the Burning Wood Fort

by Harold Jacobs

Like Andy Hope's paper, this history of Angoon clans reveals the fundamental importance of the clan in Tlingit social structure and historical consciousness. The term K̲wáan comes from the Tlingit verb "to dwell" and refers to the collective peoples and territory of clans residing in a single winter village. Harold Jacobs, whose father stems from Angoon, takes an inventory or catalogue approach to two of the major clans now residing in this ancient village by identifying major components of their social being. These include their main crests (the central symbols of social identity), their houses, names and titles (and who had them), along with other possessions. Mentioned, but not published, are items that come under the Tlingit heading "at.óow," or "owned things." For traditional Tlingits, this information is not trivial or arcane. On the contrary, knowledge of material and symbolic property was essential to the construction of personal identity and the conduct of social life. Unfortunately, too much of this traditional knowledge is becoming esoteric if not lost altogether, especially to younger generations. It is this growing ignorance that Jacobs seeks to combat.

Note from the author: *My interest in the culture of my people began as a child while visiting my grandparents' house, just two doors away from our home in Sitka. I would sit and listen to the old people tell stories of the "Killerwhale House" and the "Beaver House." In junior high school, I got started on Tlingit personal names, clan ownership and other related topics. The main source for my information in those days was my paternal grandfather, Mark Jacobs, Sr., who passed away on April 3, 1977, twelve days short of his 81st birthday.*

My first visit to Angoon was in May 1974, only long enough to visit Reverend Olson. I would not return until January 1980. Since then, I have made many trips and have sat with many elders, learning their family trees, house lineages, and songs.

Clan Conference 35

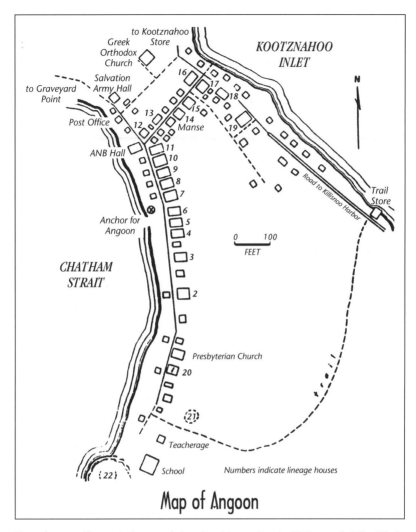

Map of Angoon

Key to Lineage Houses in Angoon: 1. Log Jam House, Aanx'aakhittaan; 2. Killer Whale Tooth House, Dakl'awedí; 3. Killer Whale House, Dakl'awedí; 4. Killer Whale House, Dakl'awedí; 5. Bear House, Teikweidí; 6. Middle of the Village House, Aanx'aakhittaan; 7. Clear Spring House, Deisheetaan; 8. Steel House, Deisheetaan; 9. Packed Solid House, Deisheetaan; 10. Raven House, Deisheetaan; 11. Trail End House, Deisheetaan; 12. Fort House, Wooshkeetaan; 13. Raven Bones House, Deisheetaan; 14. Bear Den House, lost by Teq'edi to Wooshkeetaan; 15. Valley House, Teikweidí; 16. Village End House, Deisheetaan; 17. Pit Cache House, lost by Deisheetaan, location uncertain; 18. House on Top of the Fort, originally Wooshkeetaan; 19. Basket House, Basket Bay branch of Deisheetaan; 20. Site of Edge-Around House, Aanx'aakhittaan; 21. Site of Young Tree House (Gaanax.ádi); 22. Site of Fort of Women of Gaanax.

Figure 1. Source: de Laguna, Frederica (1960) The Story of a Tlingit Community.

Those who helped educate me, some now gone, include Jimmy George Sr., William Nelson, Robert Jamestown Sr., Robert James Sr., Eddie Jack Sr., Minnie Johnson, George Jim Sr., Charlie Jim Sr., Cyrus Peck Sr., Matthew Fred Sr., Lydia George, Emma Demmert, and Joe Bennett. My greatest contributor was my grandmother, Annie Jacobs, who passed away February 10, 1989, one month short of her 89th birthday. I dedicate this writing to her, to my departed uncles and aunts: Harvey (Tliyaa Kéet), Hamilton (Gus'koos Gáan), Ernie (Gunaak'w), Franklin (Stooteix̱), and Rose (Aatoó.aat). I also dedicate this to those who remain: my father Mark Jacobs Jr. (Gusht'eiheen) and my aunt Bertha Karras (K̲'udéi).

RAVEN MOIETY

The name Xootsnoowú ("Brown Bear Fort") is sometimes wrongfully interpreted as the name for Angoon K̲wáan, this having been done by people who, my informants have told me, "Do not have a great command of the language or the history of the area."

Actually, the name comes from x̱oodzi, (which is burning wood or charred remains) not xoots (brown bear). This confusion with xoots has led to the misnomer, however widely accepted it may be, that the name of the territory means "Brown Bears' Fort." It is in fact the *Burning Wood Fort*. Xootsnoowú, however, is a descriptive name that is often applied to Admiralty Island.

Several different clans claim land on the island. The Téik̲weidí own land in Kootznahoo Inlet, the Dak̲l'aweidí own Eliza Harbor and Hood Bay, the Wooshkeetaan own Funter Bay and Hawk Inlet. The latter actually belongs to the Aak'w K̲wáan branch of the Wooshkeetaan, which own the northern half of Admiralty Island. The eastern half of the island is claimed by the Táaku K̲wáan who had a village in Seymour Canal called Siknax̱sáank'i. The rest of the area, most notably Chaik Bay, is the property of the Deisheetaan, the predominant clan of Angoon. The Goldschmidt and Haas (1998) report confirms this and that different parts of the island belonged to not only the Xoodzidaa K̲wáan but also to the Keex̱' K̲wáan, T'aak̲u K̲wáan, and Aak'w K̲wáan.

The only permanent settlement now is in Angoon, or Aangóon, being interpreted as "Town on the Portage." The clans that occupy Angoon are as follows: Deisheetaan, Kak'weidí and L'eeneidí on the Raven side and Dakl'aweidí, Teikweidí, and Wooshkeetaan on the Eagle/Wolf side. Here we will examine the social history of one clan from each side (or moiety): the Deisheetaan and the Dakl'aweidí. These are my father's and grandfather's people. I am a child of Dakl'aweidí and a grand-child of Deisheetaan.

DEISHEETAAN

Deishuhittaan — "The End of the Trail House People." There were two men, named Yéil (or Kaalkaawu) and Láxkeikw, who noticed a beaver swimming in salt water. They followed it ashore to a point at the end of a trail where they then killed the bea-ver. They decided that this is where they should build their houses and moved from their homes at Keitinjee Aan near the present ferry terminal to where Angoon is today, The first house was named Deishú Hít, or "End of the Trail House." The next house built was called Yéil Hít, or "Raven House," then the Tukka Hít or "Needlefish House." From the first house of the clan, Deishú Hít, the name was shortened from Deishuhittaan to Deisheetaan, which they are still called today.

MAIN CRESTS: Raven, Beaver

HOUSES:

1) Deishú Hít-End of the Road House

2) Yéil Hít-Raven House

3) Tukka Hít- Needlefish House

4) Shdéen Hít-Steel House

5) Goon Hít-Fresh Water Spring House

6) Yéil S'aagi Hít-Raven's Bones House

7) Tlaadein Hít-House Standing Sideways

8) Kook Hít-Pit House

9) Ts'axweil Kudei Hít-Crow's Nest House

1) Deishú Hít is the first house of the Deisheetaan. Charlie Jim (Tlingit names: Took', Shaakwáani Éesh, Lakáak'w, and Yéilk') bought the house from Jim Paul (Saanteexw). Charlie Jim Sr. was Dakl'aweidí yádi, his father, Willy Jim (Naalk'), coming from Kéet Hít (Killerwhale House) in Angoon; the mother of Willy Jim was Kaachúks, the daughter of Killisnoo Jake (Kichnáalx) of Shdéen Hít. The father of Naalk' was a Deisheetaan man named Daalkuwóox' Éesh of Deishu Hít. The mother of Charlie Jim was Sáani, the daughter of Kaachkooldeix', and a man from Kéet Ooxú Hít (Killerwhale Tooth House) named Kusax'áan.

Jim Paul (Saanteexw, Kaaxoo.átch) inherited the house from his brother, Jimmy Paul (Kaataawú). Both were Wooshkeetaan yádi, the sons of X'awulsháay (whose other names were Kootl'a.áa and Aandaxléich) of Noow Hít (Fort House) in Angoon, and his mother was Koodeishgé. The father of X'awulsháay was X'eijáak'w, a T'akdeintaan man from Yéil Kudei Hít (Raven Nest House) in Hoonah, whose father in turn was Kaagwaantaan, a man named X'aleix'w. The spokesman for the house now, however, is Garfield George (Kaasa.áxch, Kooshtoowú, Lxooda.aanyádi, Yéilk'), whose father, Jimmy George Sr. (Gus'katseix), was Deisheetaan yádi, the son of a man named L'axkéikw. Garfield's mother is Lydia George (Koodeishgé), also Dakl'aweidí yádi, whose mother, Florence Paul (X'eská), was a sister to the aforementioned Paul brothers.

2) Yéil Hít was in the joint care of Robert James Sr. (Yeilnaawú) and Joe Bennett Sr. (Áayaax). Robert James was Kaagwaantaan yádi, his father being named George James (Xáleixw) of Cháak Kudei Hít (Eagle Nest House) in Sitka. The mother of George James was X'aléixw Tláa, who was the daughter of Sitka Jack (Kichyá), a Deisheetaan man also from Yéil Hít, was the father of George James, whose own father was Teikweidí, a man named Yaanachúx. George James married Fannie Johnson (Tlingit names: Xoox Yei Leich and Aan Shaawátk'í). The father of Kichyá was Yaanachúx, Teikweidí from Xoots Hít in Angoon.

The father of Joe Bennett Sr. was Charlie Bennett (Tlingit names: Aanaxóots, Kaa.ushtí, and Haagungaax), Kaagwaantaan from Gooch Hít (Wolf House) in Sitka, who was married to Annie Bennett (Gaxtsoo); Kichgaaw, a Kiks.ádi from Kaxátjaa Hít (Shattering House [or Lively Herring House]) in Sitka, was the father of Charlie Bennett. This line can be traced back five more generations.

Robert James and Joe Bennett inherited the house from their maternal uncle Sam Johnson (Tlingit names: Áayaax and Yeilnaawú). George Johnson (K'ashaxáaw), the older brother of Sam Johnson, inherited the house from his maternal uncle Yeilnaawú. George Johnson died in 1928.

George and Sam Johnson were brothers of Annie Bennett and Fannie James. Their mother was S'eiltín, Dakl'aweidí yádi, whose father Kaalíl'i was from Keet Hít (Killerwhale House) in Angoon. His father was Til'Tlein, whose mother was Lyetu. S'eiltin was married to Shorty Johnson (Kaachgaheit'), from the Xoots Hít (Bear House) in Angoon and he was Deisheetaan yádi, the son of Aantil'ootl' from Deishú Hít (End of the Trail House) whose wife was Kaasaandu.oo.

Yéil Hít (Raven House) was built by a man named Yeilnaawú, the predecessor of Tiexyaanagút (Dick Yelnawu). Before the Raven Hat and Raven House could be dedicated Yeilnaawú died and Tiexyaangút took over and became Yeilnaawú. Yeilnaawú (born ca. 1855), Dakl'aweidí yádi, the son of Kaalíl'i of Kéet Ooxú Hít (Killerwhale Tooth House) in Angoon, was caretaker of the house from 1890 until his death in 1915. (The wife of Kaalíl'i was Kaachx'uskaayí). Dakl'aweidí yádi was a brother to S'eiltín, the mother of George and Sam Johnson, and Fannie James and Annie Bennett. They moved from a creek in Chaik Bay, known as Súkwteeya Héen. However, they should not be confused with the Sukteeneidí of Kake.

This house gets its name from the Raven, the main crest of the Deisheetaan.

3) Tuk'ka Hít is no longer standing. The proper caretaker of this house should be John Davis Jr. (Tlingit names: Kichnáalx,

Steeyan, Kanalḵú, and Keeltí Eesh). John Davis's mother is Julia Davis (Tlingit names: Xwaansan, Shaawat Tlein, and S'eistaan Tláa), the sister of Mark Jacobs Sr.

Julia Davis, Chookaneidí yádi, is the daughter of Jimmy Cohen (Chatskukoo.éesh) of X̱aatl Hít (Iceburg House) in Sitka, who was Luknax̱.ádi yádi, and her mother was Emma Cohen (S'eiltín).

Mark Jacobs Sr. inherited the house from his father-in-law John Paul (Ḵaa Tlein, Kaasa.áxch). Mark Jacobs Sr. was Teiḵweidí yádi, his father Toonax, coming from Xoots Hít (Bear House) in Angoon and the father of Toonax was also Deisheetaan. The mother of Mark Jacobs Sr. and Julia Davis was S'eiltín, Dagisdinaa yádi, whose father was T'eik of Xeitl' Hít (Thunderbird House) in Klukwan. T'eik was married to Keintéen, a Naanyaa.aayí yádi, who was the daughter of Shéiksh IV (Shaawatchooku Eesh) and a woman named S'eiltín.

This is the S'eiltín who walked across the eight coppers when she got married to Shéiksh ("Chief Shakes IV"). The Deisheetaan were hoping for more coppers and no more were added to it; this is why Mark's sister Flora (the daughter of Chatskukoo.éesh) was named Lax̱áaḵuda.oo ("Nothing Added to It"). This S'eiltín was Deikeenaa yádi, which is why Mark's most commonly known name Ḵashk'wei is a Haida name and is still used by them. The mother of this S'eiltin was also named Lax̱áaḵuda.oo and her parents were S'eiltín, and a Kaagwaantaan man from Kax̱'noowu named Taax̱shaa.

John Paul (Ḵaa Tlein, Ḵaasa.áxch), who was actually from Deishú Hít (End of the Trail House), was Wooshkeetaan yádi, and was the older brother of Jim Paul. His father, John Paul Sr., was named X'aawulhaay and his mother was named Sooxsaan.

John Paul was asked to take care of the house by Mrs. Paddy Parker (Kinle), a "clan sister" of Emma Jacobs (Séil Tin). Mrs. Parker's only brother Kalyaak'w had died which left no male heirs of age to take the house so John Paul moved from Deishú Hít to Took'ka Hít.

Daakashaan was the predecessor to John Paul. He was the father of Daaknakeen (Ike James) by a Teikweidí woman named Kaaswoot, and Deilk'i (Robert Willard Sr.) by a Wooshkeetaan woman named Aadaaneik'. He inherited the house from Kanalḵú (Joe Kennelku) who is the one who built Tuk'ḵa Hít. Kanalḵú is the paternal grandfather of Esther Littlefield of Sitka, her father Kusak'áan being the son of Kanalḵú. The name of the house refers to a needlefish; however, the house is commonly referred to as the Beaver House (S'igeidi Hit), because of the beaver screen which was once in this house.

The property was to have passed to John Davis upon the death of Mark Jacobs; however, the property is in the care of Ethel Jack (Shaḵeiwas) Kaagwaantaan yádi. Ethel Jack is the daughter of George John (Daakwtánk') of Gooch Hít (Wolf House) in Hoonah, and Mary John (Kaantoo), the daughter of Peter Tom (Náas Ḵáa), Teiḵweidí from Xoots Hít (Bear House) in Angoon, and Sophie Tom (Shdeiwteen); Ethel is from Shdeen Hít (Steel House).

4) Shdéen Hít is in the care of Emma Demmert (Aankáwtséix), Téiḵweidí yádi, whose father Náas Ḵáa (Peter Tom) came from Xoots Hít (Bear House) in Angoon, who himself was Deisheetaan yádi, the son of Jeexwanx. Mrs. Demmert is taking care of the house for her son Norman (Lk'aanáaw) who was named to replace his uncle George Davis.

George Davis (Kichnáalx, and Lk'aanáaw) was Tsaagweidí yádi, whose father, Alexander Davis (Naat'eixán) was Sitka L'uknax.adi, — and his father was a man named Gukl' from Kayaashka Hít. George Davis inherited the house from his "sister" Sophie Tom (Shdeiwteen), whose father Shtateen Éesh was Wooshkeetaan from Noow Hít. The wife of Peter Tom, Sophie inherited the house and its artifacts from Charlie Ondaynahot (Tlingit names: Aandeina.at, Xóoxwatsaa, and Kichnáalx), the Kaagwaantaan child of a man named Ḵusataan of the Eagle Nest House in Sitka. He inherited the house from his uncle Kichnáalx (Killisnoo Jake or Saginaw Jake), a Daḵl'aweidí yádi, who is the one who had the house rebuilt after the bombardment.

The name of this house is said to originate from the Killisnoo Jake, who is known to have been like steel, or had inner strength like steel.

5) Goon Hít was last in the care of Little Jack (Wool'shoox'), Yanyeidí yádi, whose father's name was Kooneik.éesh. Little Jack. He inherited the house from L'axkeikw (Jimmy Albert), the father of Jimmy George Sr. and the biological brother of (Kaajist'i Eesh) Albert Howard and Shaawatgeigéi (Elsie Frank and Mabel Willard's mother). The house was built by a man named Haatl'eekats and is an offshoot of the Steel House after the original house group got too large. After the new occupants moved in the comment was made on how quiet the place was, just like a "spring," and that is how the name came to be known as Goon Hít.

6) Yéil S'áagi Hít, an offshoot of Raven House, was last in the care of David "T" Smith (Tlingit names: Kichnáalx̱, Taatx̱áani, Héen Dei, and Kakéish). David Smith was Yanyeidí yádi. He inherited the house from his maternal uncle Jimmy Johnson (Tlingit names: Aak'w Tá and Daatk̲a sadu.axch), Dak̲l'aweidí yádi, whose father's name was Gusht'eihéen of Keet Hít (Killerwhale House) in Angoon; Gusht'eihéen was Deisheetaan yádi, whose father was Kaanaay, married to a woman named Gax̱'. Jimmy Johnson inherited the house from his brother Billy Jones. Before Jimmy Johnson, the caretaker of the house was Pete Johnson (Aanx̲isx̲áa) another brother whose wife, Martha (Aalitkwei) was the daughter of Sitka Jack, and a woman named Xootk'. The mother of Billy Jones and Jimmy Johnson was Aantkáawtseix. (This house was built as an overflow house to Shdeen Hít in the same manner as Goon Hít was.)

7) Tláadein Hít (House Standing Sideways), also in the care of Charlie John was an overflow house. Charlie John, Dak̲l'aweidí yádi, was the son of Tlek̲w Wasee and a man named Kusax̱'áan whose other wife was Kaachkooldeix'; Charlie John inherited the house from G̲áx̱wei. Kusax̱'áan, was from Keet Oox̲ú Hít (Killerwhale Tooth House) in Angoon.

8) Kook̲ Hít, no history available. Only known caretaker was K̲ushtoowú (Chaik George), the son of a Teik̲weidí man named

Kaak'w Tlein. Chaik George is the one who raised Jimmy George Sr., whose mother, Shaawat Goox, was the daughter of Kushtoowu and Shḵintután. Shḵintután was the daughter of Jeelyeix̱ and a L'eeneidi man named Haatl'i káts.

9) Ts'axweil Kúdi Hít (Crow's Nest House), no history available. The last caretaker of this house was Billy Jones (L.aangooshu, Nahóowoo, Káadei Ḵuya X̱áax'w) who was a biological brother of Jimmy and Pete Johnson. They had another brother named Billy Johnson (Aayeil). Their mother, Aakáawtseix̱, was also Daḵl'aweidí yádi, the daughter of a man named Deikeetdeitlein, and a woman named Xwaansán.

WOLF MOIETY

DAḴL'AWEIDÍ

When this group of people migrated to the coast, there were no others on the coast yet and upon seeing salt water again after they had moved into the Interior to escape the Flood, they called the tides, "Atwoogooti.áa" or "The Walking Lake." The people who had come out under the ice at Shtax'héen (Stikine River, lit. "Chewing Water") wound up in Angoon; those who went over the ice came out near Jilḵáat (Chilkat). This is why the Angoon branch owns the canoe songs composed during the migration. Their name comes from Daḵl'éiwawei.ádi or "People Who Belong to the Upper End of the Sandbar," which is the name still used today in the contracted form of Daḵl'aweidí.

Having moved into Góonx̱, now known as Eliza Harbor, they eventually moved to Tsaagwaa, Hood Bay. It was while in Tsaagwaa that a faction split off and moved over to Pybus Bay and on to Kake, a clan known as the Tsaagwa.ádi (Belonging to Tsaagwaa), more commonly known as the Tsaagweidí.

MAIN CRESTS: Killerwhale, Flicker
OTHER CRESTS: Wolf, Dog, Crane, Octopus, Murrelet.

HOUSES:

1) Kéet Hít - Killerwhale House (Also called Woochdakadin Kéet Hít - [Killerwhales Facing Away From Each Other House])
2) Tsaa Yaa.aayaanas Nak Kéet Hít - Killerwhale Chasing the Seal House (Also called Kéet Gooshi Hít - [Killerwhale Dorsal Fin House])
3) Kéet Ooxu Hít - Killerwhale Tooth House

1) Kéet Hít is in the care of Mark Jacobs Jr. (Tlingit names: Gusht'eihéen, Saa.áat', Keet wú, and Oodeishkadunéek). He is Deisheetaan yádi, the son of Mark Jacobs Sr. (Káshk'wei) of Tukka Hít in Angoon, whose father Toonax was Teikweidí from Xoots Hít in Angoon.

His mother Annie Jacobs turned control of the house over to him in 1983 during a Killerwhale clan pay-off in Angoon. Annie Jacobs (Tlingit names: Sxaalgen and Kaatukláat) was also Deisheetaan yádi, the daughter of Kaa Tlein (John Paul) of Tuk'ka Hít and Kúdei (Mary Bell Paul). Mary Bell was also Deisheetaan yádi, was the daughter of Yeilnaawú of Yéil Hít and Sxaalgen; Sxaalgen, who was Deisheetaan yádi as well, was the daughter of Kichnáalx; (Killisnoo Jake) of Shdéen Hít (Steel House) in Angoon. The wife of Killisnoo Jake was Katkatoowul.at, a sister of Gusht'eihéen.

Annie Jacobs inherited the house from her maternal uncle, Archie Bell (Tlingit names: Gusht'eihéen, Stooteix, and Daanaawú). Since Archie Bell was the brother of Mary Bell Paul (K'udei), the lineages are the same.

Archie Bell told his niece Annie Jacobs he was passing over her brother Frank Paul (Tlingit names: Kaaneitl' and Oodeishkadunéek) as caretaker for the clan property. She assumed the role as caretaker of the house in 1942 after her uncle's death.

Since Annie Jacobs lived in Sitka, she asked her "uncle" Pete Kanosh (Tlingit names: Tleeyaa Kéet and Gusht'eihéen) to stay in the house (he was actually a first cousin to Archie Bell's mother). He was not the actual caretaker of the house but was just watching it for Annie Jacobs. His father, Dick Kanosh, was Gaanax.ádi from Klawock, whose names were Lkoolkaani and Kanaash. Since Pete Kanosh was living in the house, Annie Jacobs had him given the name of Gusht'eihéen, which is the name given to every caretaker or Hít S'aatí (House Master) of Kéet Hít.

Archie Bell inherited the house from his maternal grand uncle Gusht'eihéen, a Deisheetaan yádi. This was the Gusht'eihéen who was the father of Billy Jones (L.aangooshu), Pete Johnson (Aanxisxáa), Billy Johnson (Aayéil), and Jimmy Johnson (Aak'w Tá), the four brothers who built the Killerwhale House around 1885. This was the first house of the Dakl'aweidí in Angoon.

The two killerwhales were painted on the front of the house at the same time and were commissioned by Yeilnaawú (an older one) but were done by the Yeilnaawú who was the father of Archie Bell. Because of these two killerwhales facing away from each other, the house is also called Woochdakadin Kéet Hít (Killerwhales Facing Away From Each Other House).

The head of this house before Gusht'eihéen, and before the 1882 bombardment, was his father-in-law Deikeetdeitlein.

2) Kéet Gooshi Hít, the second house of this clan, is in the care of Dan Brown Jr. (Tlingit names: Woochxkaduhaa and Gus'koos Gáan), Deisheetaan yádi, whose father Dan Brown Sr. (Lkéineek) was Dakl'aweidí yádi. Dan Brown Sr.'s father, George Brown (Neixintéik' and Tleeyaa Kéet), of Kéet Gooshi Hít in Angoon, was married to Daagunaak, Wooshkeetaan yádi, the daughter of Xáawool'shaay of Noow Hít (Fort House) whose wife was Sooxsaan. Dan Brown Jr. inherited the house from his maternal uncle Robert Jamestown Sr.

Robert Jamestown Sr. (Tlingit names: Shaakwáani and Yéildaatsée) was raised by Moses Jamestown (X'eiskeidl) of Yanxóon Hít in Angoon. His biological father, however, was Haatlí Kats' a Gaanax.ádi from T'áakú who was Dakl'aweidí yádi, his father being named Yéildaatsée. Haatlí Kats was married to Kaashda.at. Shaakwáani inherited the house from his uncle John Nelson (Tleisi Eesh) who died in 1947 and he in turn had inherited the house from his brother Kooshkí.eesh, both L'eeneidi yádi.

The builder of the house was named Yeet saa, so named because when the house was built people went in to look at the balcony that went around above the platform and "Looking Around" became the name to remember that by.

The house was later called Tsaa Yaa.ayanasnák (Tsaa Nalkeil') Kéet Hít (Killerwhale Chasing the Seal House) instead of Kéet Gooshi Hít (Killerwhale Dorsal Fin House). This was done to avoid hurting the feelings of their clan members in Klukwan who had a house by the name of Kéet Gooshi Hít, an older house than the one in Angoon.

Before the bombardment the predecessor to John Nelson was Gus'koos'kaan, the nephew of the shaman Kaadushteen.

3) The last house built was Kéet Ooxú Hít - Paul Bell (Tlingit names: Kaadushteen and Jigooní), Deisheetaan yádi, the son of Jack Bell (Daaxtinaa) who was married to Shaawat Goox, is the oldest male from this house and his sister Margaret Abbott (Tlingit names: Kak'w Taká, Kaaw aat, and Tssaagwaa Chaanukú) is the oldest female of the Killerwhale clan and therefore is also called Kéet Tláa (Killerwhale Mother). Their brother Jimmy George (Tlingit names: Wóochkaduhaa and Gus'katseix) was the last caretaker of the house.

Jimmy George, Deisheetaan yádi, was the son of Jimmy Albert (Láxkeik'w, Wooshkeetaan yádi) who was the son of Kootl'a.áa from Xeitl Hít (Thunderbird House) in Aak'w Kwáan and was married to Xoonee Sháa. Jimmy Albert was also the father of Margaret Abbott.

Jimmy George was raised by his maternal grandparents, Kooshtoowú (Chaik George) Deisheetaan from Goon Hít in Angoon; he was the son of a Teikweidí man named Kaak'w Tlein. Kooshtoowú was married to Shkintután. They were the parents of Shaawat Goox.

Jimmy George was told to move into the house by the Deisheetaan. The house was in the care of Pete Hobson (Tlingit names: Ts'een Eesh and Náaxuduyeesh). Pete Hobson inherited the house from Keeltí who was married to a woman named S'eiltín (the lineage of his S'eiltín, is not Deisheetaan but is in fact Gaanax.ádi, having been welcomed back after her ancestors had left years before). Ḵeeltí inherited the house from Kusax'áan, who was the father of Charlie John (Took') and John King (Lḵéeni) of Deishú Hít; his wives names were Tleḵw Wasee and Ḵaachkooldeix'. The last two houses were built to avert overcrowding in Kéet Hít.

REFERENCES CITED

• Goldschmidt, Walter and Theodore Haas. 1998. Haa Aaní, Our Land: Tlingit and Haida Land Rights and Use. Juneau and Seattle: Sealaska Heritage Foundation and University of Washington Press.

Herb Hope

THE KIKS.ÁDI SURVIVAL MARCH OF 1804

BY HERB HOPE

While Andy Hope is interested in the history of clan migrations and Harold Jacobs in the history of Angoon clans and their possessions, Herb Hope sharpens his focus in this paper on the history of just one event, albeit a landmark one: The Battle of 1804 between the Russians and Kiks.ádi at Sitka. And what an extraordinary and dramatic story it is, especially the long, survival march of the Kiks.ádi to Point Craven after withdrawing from their fort at Indian River. Again, the clan perspective is critical to the telling of the story. The survival march is Kiks.ádi history, a history not revealed in the written sources or even well understood by other clans. There are even slightly different versions of the event among Kiks.ádi house groups. In recent years, Herb Hope's mission has been to evaluate the oral history he learned as a boy about the Battle of 1804 by comparing it to other oral and written historical sources. In some places the stories are complementary and in other places conflicting. His findings spurred Mr. Hope to "ground truth" the story of the Kiks.ádi Survival March by re-tracing the route(s) of the marchers across Baranof Island. Indeed it became a personal quest for him, which he pursued with dogged determination despite limited funds and opposition from some quarters. In 1994, when the first part of this paper was written, Mr. Hope was still not satisfied that he had found the trail, but in 1996 he pursued a coastal route around the bays of Northwest Baranof Island and succeeded in reaching Point Craven, where the potential remains of the Kiks.ádi fort site were found and documented by archeologists. He was then satisfied that he had found the trail, but his quest continues to inspire others interested in making Tlingit history more visible and respected.

> Cháank'i yóo xat duwásaakw.
>
> Stoonookw yóo xat duwásaakw.
>
> Yéil áyá xát.
>
> Kiks.ádi áyá xát.
>
> Sheet'ká Kwáan áyá xát.
>
> X'aaká Hít xat sitee.
>
> Kaagwaantaan yádi áyá xát.

That Tlingit greeting came to you through the courtesy of Nora and Richard Dauenhauer's "Beginning Tlingit." I am just beginning to speak my own language, but I want you to know that I am aware of my Tlingit heritage—and how it has shaped my life. I want you to know that I am proud of it.

Thank you for attending this very important conference.

I am here to tell you of my efforts to retrace the route of the Sitka Kiks.ádi Survival March of 1804, an important tribal event that took place 189 years ago.

To do that I must give you some background details.

First, and foremost — the story of the Battle of Sitka of 1804 has never been told by the people most directly affected by that great battle, the Sitka Kiks.ádi people.

As brother Marks said yesterday, we, as a people, tend to shy away from the very sensitive issues. But, now that must be weighed against the loss of the Kiks.ádi side of the story for all time. It is a great story. It is a story that future generations of Tlingit people must hear.

The passing of my Kiks.ádi uncles — Andrew P. Johnson, Jimmy Williams and David Howard Sr. — signaled the end of the long line of Kiks.ádi males who knew the Kiks.ádi warrior's side of this battle.

Of my generation I believe that I am the last of the male members who heard this story as told to me by my uncles.

During the trapping seasons of 1951 and 1953 I had occasion to go fur trapping with my father, Andrew Hope, and my uncle, David Howard Sr. During the long winter nights I heard the story again and again.

This accounting then becomes all the more important because, if it is not told in public today, it may be lost for all time. Then only the slanted Russian version would survive.

The Sitka Kiks.ádi Survival March Story is a story of Tlingit courage, bravery, dedication, loyalty, honor and endurance in defense of the Kiks.ádi homeland.

It is a pleasure to offer this accounting of that great story.

We do not purposely intend to offend anyone as we tell our story but we do intend to tell the story as it had been handed down through the years. It is important to know what the Sitka Kiks.ádi thought before, during and after that great battle, 189 years ago, for it greatly influenced their behavior during the course of that battle.

According to my uncles, the Kiks.ádi thought that the Great Alliance of 1802 was still in effect. For it was the alliance that made possible the victory over the Russians in Fort Saint Michael in 1802. That is the reason for the many references to those allies in this story.

The shaman were asked time and time again:

"Is anyone coming to join us?"

"Are the war canoes on the way to join us?"

One more disclaimer before we go on with the story. This story is the Point House version of that great battle. It is but one of the six Kiks.ádi tribal houses that took part in this battle. The six house groups were:

1. The House on the Point
2. Clay House
3. Strong House
4. Herring House

5. Steel House

6. House Inside the Fort

It is important to remember that each house group fought as a military unit under their own house chief.

It is true that the clan had chosen Katlian (K̲'alyaan) as war chief over Shk̲'oowulyéil—but each house was an independent military unit and saw the battle from that perspective.

This accounting is dedicated to the memory of the brave warriors who fought this battle and to the non-combatant old men and women, infants and children who were the casualties of this major confrontation between the Tlingit Indians and the European intruders who were invading their lands.

The loss of life was extremely heavy. Warriors and civilians alike suffered losses to cannon fire for the first time in their history.

We salute them as we remember them.

The idea of this recounting started innocently enough.

In 1987 I attended the Alaska Native Brotherhood Convention in Sitka and, as usual, I went to attend the luncheon that is always hosted by the Sitka Kiks.ádi, as the original Sitka people, to welcome the Convention. But this year was different, there were no male Kiks.ádi elders to welcome the ANB and ANS delegates to Sitka and to briefly speak of our clan leaders and history.

Instead, several female speakers rose to speak in a manner I had never heard before—they were apologizing for our part in the war of 1804. They even admitted to our people killing the young infants before retreating into the hills. In short they were telling the Russian version of the story.

I rose to object and said,

When we speak of our history we must speak with pride, for only we know the true story of our participation in the War of 1804. We do not need to quote anything the Russians had to say about the battle.

Another thing, the Sitka Kiks.ádi retreat from Fort Shís'gi Noow was not a headline military retreat as you have just said—rather it was a *survival march* through our own backyard to a planned destination.

The story you have just told sounds like the story only a very disapproving Presbyterian Minister would tell.

Maybe it is time for us to reenact the Sitka Kiks.ádi Survival March so we can properly tell our story with pride and honor.

I sat down to a strong round of applause.

And so began my efforts to reenact the Kiks.ádi Survival March of 1804.

I began by questioning all the elders who would listen to me. I asked, "What was the route your house group took during the Survival March?"

I asked many people but no one could give me a specific answer.

I went out and bought all the nautical charts and topographical maps of the north end of Baranof Island and studied them carefully. When they did not give enough detail about the interior of the island, I located all the aerial photos I could find of the entire north end of Baranof Island.

I traced all possible routes and combinations of routes from Sitka to Hanus Bay and began to eliminate them one by one.

I wrote letters to everyone I could think of who might know something about the Survival March. I didn't really expect anyone to answer, and I was right. I did not receive a single response.

I actively solicited support for an effort I intended to launch in September of 1988. Twelve people, including several ladies, said they would participate in all or part of the effort.

I read all the books I could get my hands on concerning the history of events leading to the Battle of Sitka of 1804.

PRELUDE TO THE BATTLE OF SITKA, 1804

The European fur traders arrived in Southeast Alaska in the late 1770s. The fabulous sea otter's pelt was the prize sought by the daring fur traders.

The Russians appeared, coming down from the north, after depleting the sea otter stocks in the Aleutian Islands, Cook Inlet and Prince William Sound.

The English appeared from the south after they depleted the natural stocks of sea otter around Vancouver Island and Queen Charlotte Islands.

The Yankees were late comers into the fur trade, but they arrived in force in the late 1770s. They were the first to trade muskets and gunpowder to the Tlingit Indians in exchange for the valuable sea otter pelts.

The Russians established forts at Yakutat and Sitka in an attempt to gain control of Southeast Alaska. The Hudson Bay Company made its move and some historians say that they called the northern Tlingit Tribes to a meeting in Angoon in 1801. At this secret meeting they offered muskets and gunpowder to the Tlingits in exchange for exclusive fur trading rights.

A plan was agreed upon. The tribes would unite for an attack against the Russian Fort Saint Michael at Old Sitka. The Hudson Bay Company would supply the muskets and gunpowder. The attack would take place in the spring of 1802.

Some historians say that the warriors from the following villages took part in the Battle of 1802: Sitka, Angoon, Kake, Hoonah, Auke Bay, and Klukwan.

The same historians say that the attack was planned to take place while the Russian sailing ships were away in Kodiak.

The attack was a complete success.

Fort Saint Michael was completely destroyed and the warriors returned home victorious.

Soon after the battle, the Sitka Kiks.ádi shaman foresaw the return of the Russian sailing ships to seek revenge for the loss of Fort Saint Michael.

Shaman Stoonookw was adamant about the need for a new fort capable of withstanding cannon fire. Against strong opposition he prevailed and the fort was under construction in 1803.

The Sitka Kiks.ádi prepared themselves for total war.

In August of 1804, the Russians, under the command of Baranof, returned in their three small sailing ships along with 400 Aleut sea otter hunters in bidarkas. They were joined by the Russian frigate *Neva*, a 200-foot-long, three-masted sailing ship that weighed 350 tons. It had 14 cannons and was manned by a crew of 50 professional sailors.

The *Neva* was of English design and construction. It was a new ship and state-of-the-art in warships of that era.

Neither side rushed into battle. The Sitka Kiks.ádi sent messages to their allies of 1802, but did not receive any affirmative replies or commitments.

While awaiting replies from their allies of 1802, the Sitka Kiks.ádi devised a battle plan.

In a surprise move the Kiks.ádi appointed a new war chief, Katlian, who replaced Shḵ'awulyéil, leader of the successful war of 1802.

Each of the six Kiks.ádi house groups quickly rallied around their own "house chief." As they had done down through the ages, all of the house groups would fight as military units under their own house chiefs, but under the direction of the war chief and his shaman.

The plan was simple. The Kiks.ádi would test the strength and intentions of the Russians at Noow Tlein, the fort on Castle Hill, then fall back on the new fort called "Shís'gi Noow," or "Second Growth Fort," located at the high water line near "Ḵaasdahéen" or the stream now called Indian River. This fort was roughly two hundred feet square and approximately one thousand logs were used in its construction.

The fort had been constructed there to take advantage of the long gravel beach flats that extend far out into the bay. It was hoped that the distance would reduce the effect of cannon fire from the Russian ships.

Once settled in Fort Shís'gi Noow, the Kiks.ádi would use delaying tactics to gain time for the northern tribes to arrive. The shaman were consulted to see if the northern tribes were on their way to Sitka. The shaman reported back—they could not see any of their allies traveling toward Sitka. They continued to see a "dark force" in the future.

The Kiks.ádi house chiefs and their shaman met again and again. It was apparent that time was running out. The northern allies would not make it in time. The house chiefs considered the situation. The Russians demanded that the Kiks.ádi surrender. The house chiefs were unanimous in their conclusion. "We cannot surrender and become the slaves of the Russians. We will fight alone if we have to!" The decision was made—We will fight alone.

The entire reserve of gun powder was located in a small cave on one of the small islands in Jamestown Bay, one half mile away.

An elite crew was picked to go to get the gunpowder and bring it to Shís'gi Noow. The crew included the high caste young men from each house—men who were being groomed to be the future leaders of those houses. A respected elder was chosen to lead the party.

The gun powder was picked up and, in the spirit of the occasion, the crew decided not to wait for darkness to cover their return to Fort Shís'gi Noow; instead they would return immediately in broad daylight.

The Russians opened fire as soon as they came into range. The young warriors fired back with their muskets. Suddenly there was a great explosion. When the smoke cleared away the canoe was gone.

Gone!

The entire canoe was gone. The entire reserve gun powder supply was gone. The elite young men from every house were gone. The respected elder leader was gone. A tragic loss before the battle was fully underway.

The next day Baranof launched his attack.

DAY ONE

Baranof landed his force on the beach directly in front of the fort without consulting Captain Lisianski or making use of the *Neva*'s cannon to bombard the fort.

Baranof insisted on leading the attack.

The Russians advanced up the beach behind the four hundred Aleut sea otter hunters who were used as light infantry.

The Kiks.ádi shaman had foreseen this frontal assault and had advised Katlian to have the Kiks.ádi warriors withhold their fire until the Aleut hunters were directly beneath the fort walls.

The Kiks.ádi warriors displayed strong military discipline by withholding their fire, as instructed, until the Aleut hunters reached the fort walls.

Then they opened fire with volley after volley over the heads of the Aleut hunters into the ranks of the Russians who were just coming into range.

The Aleuts broke rank and began a retreat west to the beaches where their bidarkas were waiting. They were pursued by the younger warriors who made a dash from behind the fort into the confusion on the beach.

It was a calm day and the battlefield was soon covered by a heavy layer of gun smoke, making it difficult for either side to see what was going on.

Amid the smoke of the battlefield Katlian and several warriors sprang up from Ḵaasdahéen and attacked the Russians from their rear. The battle flowed down the beach.

The Kiks.ádi warriors charged out of Shís'gi Noow and pursued the retreating Russians. The Kiks.ádi saw Baranof fall in battle. They saw his troops carry him from the battlefield. Just as the Russians reached the water's edge the *Neva's* cannon opened fire, covering the last of the Russian retreat.

The Russians were forced to leave their small cannon behind on the beach as they boarded their launches and left the battlefield.

The battle was over.

The Russians had launched their attack confident of victory, now they had barely escaped total defeat. Their losses were heavy.

The Kiks.ádi warriors rejoiced.

DAY TWO

Baranof's battlefield wounds prevented him from leading the battle. Lisianski took command, but he had no immediate plan of action other than to bombard the fort from his ships. By late morning Lisianski began a cannon bombardment that lasted all day long as he attempted to find the range of fort Shís'gi Noow.

In the early afternoon the Russians stopped their cannon fire and sent a messenger ashore under a flag of truce.

The Kiks.ádi were surprised to learn that the message was a demand for them to surrender. They rejected it out of hand.

They sent back a counter-demand that the Russians surrender. It was rejected by the Russians.

The cannon fire resumed, but it stopped at nightfall.

The Kiks.ádi were on the alert all day long but the Russians made no attempt to land forces to launch another ground attack. After dark the Kiks.ádi met to consider the situation. Each house group was short of gunpowder. Too much gun powder had been used the day before.

The lack of a Russian ground attack convinced them that the Russians were unable to launch another attack. They all believed that the Russians suffered too many losses the day before.

The shaman were consulted to see if they could see the northern tribes, but they reported no change in the situation. No warriors were on the way to join them in Sitka.

As a side note, let me say that it is my opinion that Captain Lisianski acted very, very cautiously throughout this battle. The battle was his to win if he took decisive action.

He chose, instead, to act cautiously. He wrote a better battle than he fought. He did not want to endanger his main mission, which was to be the first Russian to circumnavigate the world—a job he had been commissioned to do by the Czar of all the Russias.

Now, on day two of the battle, the lack of gun powder and the failure of the northern tribes to come to the assistance of the Kiks.ádi made victory seem less likely. In fact, the possibility of defeat on the battlefield had to be seriously considered.

Holding the fort without gun powder looked more and more like a lost cause. Desperate times need desperate measures. The house chiefs all agreed on one thing—delaying tactics were in order. Every possible method of delaying a Russian attack had to be used to give the northern tribes time to arrive.

In the free-ranging discussion someone proposed leaving the battlefield and marching to the north. Abandon Shís'gi Noow. Live to fight another day!

We cannot be defeated on the battlefield if we are not on that battlefield to be defeated.

A committee was appointed to consider the pros and cons of a survival march to the north. A march on foot.

Actually, this was a reasonable alternative, for the Tlingit people were a strong, healthy people who walked everywhere they went, usually carrying a heavy load. When not walking they paddled their canoes wherever they went.

DAY THREE

The *Neva* resumed the naval bombardment. The second day of the naval bombardment started at sunrise. The Kiks.ádi responded by using more delaying tactics; they offered a truce, hostage exchanges, promises of more talks, and held out the possibility of surrender.

In the meantime the Survival March got underway. The elderly, accompanied by their young grandchildren, started the trek to Gajaa Héen (Old Sitka).

At nightfall, the House Chiefs met again. This time the discussion concerned the actual Survival March, and the details were arranged. The elderly and their grandchildren had already moved out. They were followed by the young mothers with infant children.

Now the plans were laid out for the rest of the clan to follow. The meeting broke up as each family had to organize itself for the long march.

A second meeting was called by the younger house chiefs and house chiefs-to-be.

"Survival is not enough," said the young chiefs. "We must plan for our return to Sheet'ká. We must blockade Peril Straits. No Tlingit must be allowed to trade with the Russians in Sheet'ká. We must return to Sheet'ká for the herring egg harvest in Sheet'ká and to all our fish camps next summer. All Tlingits must know that the Kiks.ádi still own Sheet'ká."

The older chiefs quickly agreed to the plan.

Preparation began in earnest for the Survival March.

The House Chiefs told their people, "Take only what is absolutely needed. For we will do as marchers have done down through the ages. We will eat off the land as we go."

DAY FOUR

The day began with a naval bombardment of cannon fire.

During pauses in the cannon fire the Russians made offers to the Kiks.ádi to end the battle. The Kiks.ádi rejected all offers.

The cannon fire resumed.

Late in the afternoon the Kiks.ádi made an offer to accept the Russian terms. They will leave Shís'gi Noow the next day.

The Kiks.ádi made this offer to prevent the Russians from attacking while the clan was involved in the last minute preparations to start the Survival March.

A special signal was arranged to indicate that the Kiks.ádi were ready to leave.

After dark the Kiks.ádi gathered for the last time in Shís'gi Noow. The remaining elders thanked everyone for defending the homeland of the Kiks.ádi against a hated, but formidable, enemy.

The House Chiefs formally addressed the people to thank them for their bravery in battle and for agreeing to go on the Survival March to the north.

The clan gathered together for one last song in Shís'gi Noow to signal the Russians that they were ready to leave.

It was a extremely sad song sung from the heart of everyone in the fort.

It expressed their pain and anguish at the outcome of this great battle, it expressed their grief at the loss of Shís'gi Noow and Noow Tlein, their tribal houses, their many canoes and their ceremonial regalia.

It gave vent to all the grief they still felt for the loss of so many friends and relatives. They remembered the lost warriors who were their grandfathers, fathers, uncles, husbands, brothers and sons as well as the grandmothers, mothers, aunts, wives, sisters and daughters who died in the naval bombardment.

They remembered the young house chiefs-to-be who died when the canoe carrying the gunpowder blew up.

The warriors mourned the loss of another chance to fight hand to hand combat with their hated enemies.

The song ended with a loud drum roll and a wail of anguish.

The Kiks.ádi made their final preparations and left Shís'gi Noow for the last time.

Where did they go?

How long did it take?

We do know that a strong Rear Guard stayed behind and harassed the Russians for several weeks to confuse them about the direction the Kiks.ádi had taken.

The legends and stories about the Survival March differ a great deal. No one knows the exact route for sure.

I researched the stories and interviewed many of the elders before reaching the conclusion that the only way to know for certain would be to "walk the walk" as the young people say.

THE 1988 EFFORT

In 1988 I secured a small grant from the Humanities Forum that paid my round trip Anchorage to Sitka plus a small amount I thought I would need for a support vessel. Bill Brady offered his boat at no cost.

Prospective participants dropped out one-by-one as the departure date neared.

Only my brother Fred and I remained on the departure date.

We set the date of departure for Sept. 26—the same date the actual event took place.

We chose the Indian River route to Katlian Bay.

We estimated it to be nine miles distance and we thought we could do it in one long day.

We left early in the day carrying light packs and walked all day in a heavy rainfall.

We could not locate the bear trail that is supposed to go up the saddle between the Three Sisters and the Old Sitka mountain range.

We turned west and began to climb a 2,400 foot mountain even though we knew we could not possibly make it to the top before dark.

We climbed to the 2,200 foot level and made camp.

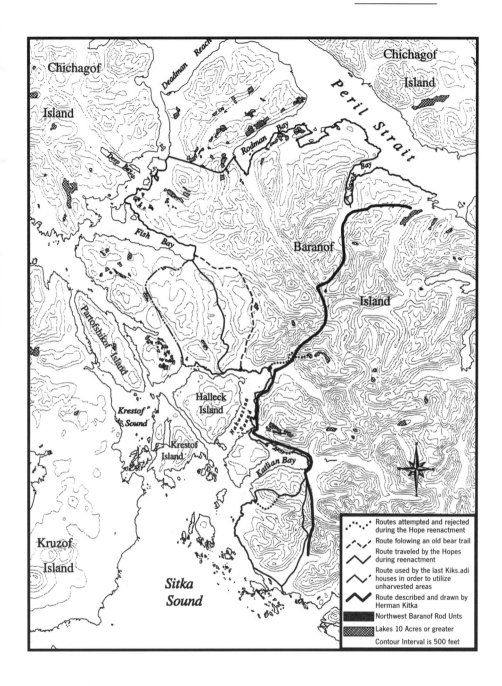

The Sitka Kiks.ádi Survival March Trail

It was too wet for a fire. We settled for an emergency camp and prepared for a long wet night. I strung a 100 foot nylon cord from our emergency shelter to a small tree about ninety feet away. Whenever we got too cold we jumped up and walked or ran between the trees until we warmed up again. We did that all night.

We rose at daybreak and climbed the remaining distance to the top of the mountain.

We continued along toward Katlian Bay on the alpine tops.

We descended into Katlian Bay down a route I knew years ago. We rapidly moved down the mountain until we ran into an area that had been "clear cut." We spent the entire afternoon crossing that clear cut.

We arrived in Katlian Bay and found large numbers of dog salmon still in the river and still in fairly good condition.

A Coast Guard helicopter flew over us when we were less than 300 yards from the beach. Apparently it was looking for us, but we signaled him that we were alright and heading for the beach.

We arrived on the beach exhausted, soaking wet, hungry and about ten pounds lighter than when we left Sitka two days before.

We conferred with Bill Brady and agreed with his advice to go back to Sitka to confer with the elders.

We did meet with the elders and we agreed that it would be better to postpone any further effort for one year.

THE 1989 EFFORT

Andy Hope took a serious interest in the 1989 effort and secured a grant from Sealaska to record our efforts.

Labor Day weekend was chosen in order to make it possible to include more participants. The Coast Guard was alerted to our route. The Sitka Fire Department loaned us a good radio.

The 1989 party consisted of Herbert Hope, Fred Hope, Harold Kitka (representing the Eagles), Tom Thornton (a young anthropologist), Bill Brady (on the support vessel), and Ralph Brady (as deckhand on the support vessel).

After a brief ceremony at the site of Shís'gi Noow that included young Tlingit dancers and singers, and several speakers, we were off.

We chose the route from the Sitka National Monument to Halibut Point then on to Gajaa Héen (Old Sitka). A distance of 7 miles for the first day's efforts.

My sister Ellen Hayes, my friend Alfred Gray and his daughter walked with us to Gajaa Héen. We arrived at 3:00 p.m. in time to join a tribal picnic being held in our honor. We camped overnight at the campgrounds and departed early the next morning.

We climbed a 2,500 foot mountain then walked along the mountain tops toward Katlian Bay. We descended into Katlian Bay where we were met by our support vessel. We moved two miles across the bay and set up camp at Cedar Cove.

The next day we crossed the peninsula that separates Katlian Bay and Nakwasina Bay. We lost some time when we got mixed up with another clear cut area.

We arrived in Nakwasina and began the long walk to the north along the gravel beaches that line the shore. As agreed upon, Bill Brady soon arrived and picked us up and took us to the head of the bay. We have walked these beaches many times and I didn't think that we needed to do it again.

We landed in the main river and headed for the mountain passes on the west side of the valley before making camp for the night.

The next day we began our climb toward what we hoped were mountain passes. In a driving rainfall and under heavy cloud cover we made a wrong turn and headed up the wrong valley.

After climbing all day we reached a lake at elevation 1,927 feet. We tried to find a way around the lake but we could not make it past any of the cliffs that fall directly into the lake.

The next day we called it off and returned to the beach. We were out of annual leave time and had to get back to our jobs. We were satisfied that this was not the route taken by our people in 1804.

After returning to Anchorage I thought this over and decided to build a scale model of this area of the island to see what kind of terrain lay between Nakwasina and Hanus Bay. The scale is one quarter inch to each 500 feet. The model started out to be 2 feet by 2 feet but has since grown to be 4 feet wide by 5 feet long.

THE 1990 EFFORT

The 1990 effort was centered around finding a route through the west fork of the Nakwasina River.

Topographical maps show a very steep, narrow valley slowly enlarging to drain a very large alpine valley up to six miles wide. We would try to find a way through the narrow funnel where the river joins the main Nakwasina River.

Our cousin, Louie Howard, volunteered to be our support vessel and brother Fred and I departed on the Labor Day weekend.

We landed in Nakwasina and proceeded directly to our destination. It was very steep going. We ran into waterfall after waterfall. We pressed on, but it kept getting steeper and steeper, we ran into cliffs, landslides, heavy brush, and steep ridges. It was hard going. It rained without letup. We searched every possible trail or hint of a trail. We ran into more cliffs and steeper landslides.

After a hard day of climbing we ran into a waterfall which we could not find a way around. It was too steep and rocky. We camped there overnight and made our way back to the beach the next day.

We were satisfied that this, too, was not the route taken by our people in 1804.

1991

No effort was undertaken in 1991 due to the serious illness my wife, Hilda Lorraine, was suffering.

THE 1992 EFFORT

My wife passed away in July of 1992. To help overcome my grief I traveled to Sitka to try again to find the route taken by our people in 1804.

We arrived in early August. Boyd Didrickson of the Herring House was captain of our support vessel. We received a cash donation from the Sitka Tribe to pay for gas.

Brother Fred and Harold Kitka were not able to get away from their jobs so only my son Doug and I were left to make this year's effort.

We traveled to Humpy Creek in Nakwasina pass and entered the woods there. Our intention was to see if it is possible to travel from Nakwasina Pass to Fish Bay through the low valley that separates them.

We had bad luck right from the beginning—we ran into a logged off area that we couldn't get around. We ended up climbing over a hill (1,485 ft.) to get around the clear cut. That ate up the first day. We decided to enjoy the remainder of the day and set up camp on the mountain top.

The next day we began our descent of the mountain's north face and ran into another clear cut area.

The entire morning was lost as we forced our way through the clear cut.

When we came out of the clear cut we ran into a series of old logging roads. We followed them west till we got to a point where we could see all the possible routes to Fish Bay. The most logical route was to our east between two clear cut areas.

I had not been able to properly train for this year's effort and I knew I wouldn't be able to climb a second mountain in two day's time.

I radioed ahead to Boyd in Fish Bay telling him of my decision and turned and headed back to Nakwasina Pass.

Even though I was forced to turn back again I was feeling good. This route looked likely. A group of one thousand people could make it through here easily compared to the mountain passes above Nakwasina River.

THE NEXT EFFORT

Our next try will closely follow on the heels of the 1992 effort. We will attempt to follow the ridge line from Nakwasina into Fish Bay.

We will then follow the north shore of Fish Bay to Sergius Narrows.

We will then follow the shoreline to Rose Channel then cross the peninsula that separates Rose Channel from Rodman Bay.

From Rodman Bay we will follow the shoreline to Appleton Cove and on to Saook Bay.

In closing let me simply say that we held great respect for our ancestors as we retraced their footsteps.

Many who told me, "Oh, they went over the mountains," could not climb Gavin Hill or Mt. Verstovia much less help their grand mother up the mountain—then climb dozens of mountains on the way to Hanus Bay.

My efforts to re-trace the Survival March route has changed my life. I now try hard to stay in physical condition. I walk five miles a day after work, more on weekends.

I have changed my diet. No salt or sugar. No dairy products. No fried foods. No foods with preservatives. No coffee.

I train intensely for weeks before each expedition.

We come from a strong people.

We carry that strength in our genes.

No obstacle is too great for us to overcome.

Like our ancestors we must plan before we act.

Then act with conviction.

POSTSCRIPT

As noted in the introduction, Mr. Hope continued to research and retrace probable Kiks.ádi Survival March routes until 1996, when he successfully navigated a coastal trail to Hanus Bay and, with vessel support, crossed Peril Strait to the spot near Point Craven, where the Kiks.ádi settled at a fort called Chaatlk'aanoow ("Little Halibut Fort"or "Fort on Top of the Halibut"). Archeologists believe they have found the remains of this site, and Herb Hope is satisfied that the story of what happened during the Kiks.ádi Survival March can now be told from a Kiks.ádi perspective. Here is that story.

And so the four day long Battle of Sitka of 1804 came to an end.

The Sheet'ká Kiks.ádi were now in the process of executing a tactical retreat from this battlefield for three reasons. First, to keep their women and children from becoming slaves to the Russians. Second, to keep their warriors alive to fight another day. Third, to leave this battlefield with their honor intact.

Only the following day would tell if the Russians had the courage to end the battle in their favor by pursuing the Kiks.ádi into the deep woods.

When the song ended the people sat together in small groups comforting one another for a short time. Then they checked their packs and gear one last time, making sure no unnecessary items were included, for they were keenly aware that they were expected to live off the land on this march.

In spite of the emotion and excitement of the last few hours many managed to catch a few hours of sleep. When the first hint of daybreak appeared the sentries went silently from bedroll to bedroll shaking everyone awake. The people rose, quietly picked up their packs and moved up Kaasdaa Héen (Indian River). They moved fast for they were the able-bodied members of the clan.

One house group went up the Indian River valley to cross over the mountains to Katlian Bay as they had planned, but the rest of the people headed north along the coastal trail toward Halibut Point.

The people marched at a steady pace for they knew that a strong rear guard, composed of the best Kiks.ádi warriors, protected them from any sudden attack by the Anooshee. They also knew that sharp-eyed young lookouts were up on Harbor Mountain and Gavin Hill keeping an eye on the Russian ships. Fleet young runners stood by the lookouts, ready to run to warn the marchers if the Russian ships lifted anchor and began a search for the missing Tlingit people.

It is said that the rear guard action was so strong and effective that the Russians were convinced that the main body of the Sheet'ká Kwaan were still lurking in the woods somewhere behind Sheet'ká ready to do battle again.

Thus the people were free to march without fear of the Russian ships. By early evening they arrived in G̲ajaa Héen (Old Sitka) and joined the elders, women and children who waited for them there.

KATLIAN BAY

From G̲ajaa Héen (Old Sitka) the people took several different routes up the mountains that separate Old Sitka from Katlian Bay till they reached the ridge tops, which they followed, continuing eastward until they could descend to the head of Katlian Bay. As they began to arrive at the bay in the late afternoon and on into the evening, they searched for and rejoined their own house groups. The main camp was set up near the old smokehouses in the southeast corner of the bay.

Early the next morning the men went to work harvesting dog salmon, flounder, and crab, while the ladies and children were busy picking berries and tidal flat grass roots. By nightfall they were all enjoying a big cookout of their catch and pickings of the day.

While they were eating, a runner arrived with this message from the rear guard forces: "The Russians are taking apart Shís'g̲i Noow and are towing the salvaged logs to Noow Tlein. There is no pursuit." The shaman were pleased to hear this news for they had predicted, on the eve of their departure from Shís'g̲i Noow: "We see it clearly, the Anooshee will not leave the safety of their ships to follow us into the deep woods."

After the big cookout the House Chiefs met to choose the routes they would each take from Katlian to Fish Bay. The elders advised, "As in the migration stories it is important for us to walk as families, but within the house groups. We must avoid taking identical routes whenever possible. We must not follow too closely behind the house group in front of us. We must walk at a steady pace, but we must also take advantage of all the food we can find along the way including late salmon, trout, ducks, geese, berries of all kinds, shellfish, grass roots, plant roots, tree bark, deer and bear."

The House Chiefs decided that they would follow each other into Nakwasina; there they would split into three parties to cross the broad peninsula that separates Nakwasina from Fish Bay, the better to forage and hunt. They would meet again in Fish Bay to choose the routes they would take from that point on to Hanus Bay.

Once they were underway messengers from each house would keep in daily contact with the house group directly in front of them and the house group directly behind them.

Lest there be any doubts, the House Chiefs also reaffirmed their decision to remain on a full war footing. The Kiks.ádi were still at war with the Anooshee. Katlian would remain as War Chief.

As the meeting came to an end, Katlian reminded the people, "The rear guard warriors are still in action around Sheet'ká and they shall remain in action for ten or twenty more days before coming to join us. Take heart—no one is pursuing us, walk with a steady pace, this march is our survival march."

After the cook-out the badly wounded warriors announced to their relatives that they would not be going on with the main body, but would stay behind and winter in Katlian Bay rather than be a hindrance to the marchers along the way.

Next, several of the elderly stepped forward and said, "We are very old and it is not right for us to expect you to wait for us. We will stay here and winter with the wounded; there is salmon in these streams till far into the winter. Do not fear for our well being. We will be all right. Come and get us in the springtime. We will be waiting."

Early the next morning the younger members of the families of the wounded and the elders were out gathering firewood. They wanted to give them a head start on the winter wood supply. They worked all day.

Other family members made repairs to the living quarters, working far into the night. When darkness fell the families got together for a time of fellowship with their elders. There was good food to eat, stories to tell and tribal songs to sing.

The march got underway again with the morning light. There was no panic. There was no fear. The Russians were far away in Sheet'ká. When it was time to leave, the house groups left Katlian Bay according to their social ranking in the Sheet'ká village. They were still the Sheet'ká Kiks.ádi people. They still had a very special social order. Life still had a purpose.

DAXÉIT (NAKWASINA SOUND)

In one long day they moved across the rugged north shore of Katlian Bay and on into Cedar Cove. They set up camp near the stream in the northwest corner of the cove. Scouts immediately went ahead to mark the trail across the muskegs to Nakwasina Sound.

Early the next morning they followed the marked trail across the narrow peninsula into Nakwasina Sound. When they reached Nakwasina Sound, they turned north and followed the gravel beaches toward the fish camps at the head of the bay. Some families made it all the way to the fish camps while others stopped and camped along the way.

Dog salmon and silver salmon were in abundance at the head of the bay as was usual at that time of the year. Soon they were enjoying another feast of fresh salmon.

After a short rest the people departed from Daxéit (Nakwasina) according to the prearranged routes they had agreed upon in Katlian Bay. Three different routes were to be followed as they crossed the 12-mile wide peninsula north toward Fish Bay. They moved slowly through this area for it was the deer migration season. The deer had only recently moved off their summer feeding grounds high in the alpine regions of the interior mountains. Now they were slowly moving down into their winter feeding grounds on the low hills near the ocean. There were many deer in the area and hunting was good.

FISH BAY

When they arrived in Fish Bay, they set up their main camp near the smokehouses of the hunter's camp located in the north corner of the bay close to the main river. They stayed long enough to smoke and to partially dry their fresh deer meat for use on the trail that lay ahead.

Once underway again they followed the long gravel beaches nine miles west to Schultz Cove. They rested there overnight. The next morning they entered the woods, turned north and followed the low ridge just above the shoreline of Sergius Narrows to Bear Bay. From Bear Bay they followed the shoreline into Little Bear Bay. The first two house groups passed right through this area in order to leave untouched shellfish resources for those traveling behind.

ROSE CHANNEL

The lead house group moved right on to Rose Channel where they set up camp near the large stream. Their hunters moved on to the low muskegs and hills to hunt the large herds of deer that are in this area during this time of year.

It is said that one family turned north to winter at Deadmans Reach. War Chief Katlian tried to talk them out of it, but they left anyway. They had a hunting camp in that area and were confident that they could winter-over very well there.

When the lead house group left Rose Channel they moved into the woods, headed east until they found the old bear trail and followed it across the narrow peninsula to the stream draining into the southeast corner of Rodman Bay. The bear trail followed the stream into the bay. The scouts left a clearly marked trail for the other house groups to follow.

RODMAN BAY

The walk from Rose Channel to Rodman Bay was an easy hike of approximately ten miles. When they reached the beach in Rodman Bay they moved on to the head of the bay without stopping and set up camp there. From this point, all the way up to Hanus Bay most of the traveling would be on the beaches. So after a short rest they were underway again, walking along the beach to Appleton Cove eight miles to the north.

From Appleton Cove they followed the rocky outer beach toward Saook Bay, harvesting some of the abundant shellfish as they moved along.

HANUS BAY

The final leg of the journey was along the beach from Saook Bay to Point Moses. Compared to many places along the way this was easy walking along good gravel beaches. Occasionally there were short stretches of boulder strewn beaches but most of the beaches were wide and gently sloping.

The first house group arrived at Moses Point without fanfare, then moved on to their main destination—the Lake Eva river in Hanus Bay.

Early that morning the house chief had sent his runners back to contact the houses still coming up. The runners returned late that evening and reported, "The people are scattered out five or six days marching time behind us."

A quick survey was enough to determine that there was no sign of recent human activity in Hanus Bay. This was disappointing news. Now they had to find a way to alert their possible neighbors, nine miles across the open water of Peril Strait.

THE BONFIRE

While waiting for the other house groups to arrive the people began to build a large signal bonfire they hoped would be seen by the village lookout at Chaatlk'aanoow (Fort on top of the Halibut), or one of the other three or four village forts near Point Craven and Morris Reef, nine to twelve miles away on Chichagof Island.

Because of the October rain and storms they had to wait for a clear evening before lighting the signal fire. As each House group arrived they marked a tree near Moses Point to commemorate the occasion of their arrival at the end of this great survival march. They also marked a young hemlock tree on three sides to locate the spot where the signal fire was prepared.

A clear night arrived and the people could see the other shore nine miles away. The twenty-foot high signal fire was started and after it was burning good, small bull pine trees were lifted on long poles and placed on top of the signal fire. The fire would flare-up every time the bull pine trees ignited. This was done so that anyone who saw the fire could tell that it was a man-made signal fire.

The people were happy to see the bonfire burning so brightly, especially when the bull pine trees were placed near the top and they flared-up so brightly. A spontaneous celebration began to take place. It was unbelievable, but from somewhere a drum began to beat. Others began to keep time by beating small hand sticks while others beat larger beach logs with heavy sticks. Singers joined the drummers. More people joined the singers in song after song of traditional Tlingit songs of celebration and thanksgiving.

One by one the clan elders rose to speak. In a very formal manner reserved for great occasions, they thanked the people for enduring the hardships of the trail and for helping each other out along the way. They called out the names of their grandchildren and thanked them for their help on the many days on the trail. They spoke with pride on how much their young grandchildren had learned about the ways of the trail.

It is said that a Point House elder spoke and said,

Always remember that you are the Sheet'ká Kiks.ádi people.

You and you alone carry the proud names of our noble ancestors.

You are worthy of the great names you carry for in this battle and on this survival march you have added glory to those proud names.

The clan will always remember that it was you who fought the hated Anooshee in defense of the homeland of the Tlingit people, when none of our allies came to our assistance.

It was you who spilled your blood rather than disgrace our people by surrendering to the hated Anooshee.

It was you who fought for and held Shisg'i Noow for those many days.

It is you who turned back the Anooshee attack on Shisg'i Noow.

It was you who knocked down Baranof and saw him carried from the battlefield.

It was you who endured the many days of cannon fire in Shisg'i Noow.

It was you who endured the long march from Shisg'i Noow to Hanus Bay in order for our tribe to survive with honor.

We give a very special thank you to our sons and daughters— the Kiks.ádi yádi. You are all of the Eagle moiety. We are proud that you fought by our side in our time of need. We will never forget it. The Kaagwaantaan, the Wooshkeetaan, the Teikweidí, the Shangukeidí and all the other Eagle clans that you represent will long honor your names for the valor you have shown.

Gunalchéesh, ho, ho.

Now we must continue to be strong as we face the future.

We have much to do before we can return to our ancient homeland in Sheet'ká.

The blockade must begin now.

We will return to our homeland when the time is right.

THE CANOES ARRIVE

The next morning several canoes could be seen crossing from the other shore.

Tradition says that it was the Angoon people who came to the rescue of the Sheet'ká Kiks.ádi. We had many arranged marriages with the Angoon people to settle boundary disputes over where Kiks.ádi territory ended and where Angoon territory began.

Some say it was the Deisheetaan who manned the rescue canoes.

To this day the Kiks.ádi hold the Angoon people in high regard for coming to our assistance in a time of great need.

CHAATLK'AANOOW

The Sitka Kiks.ádi promptly took over the abandoned fort called Chaatlk'aanoow near Point Craven. They re-roofed the old tribal houses with new bark strips and went to work re-enforcing the old fort atop the high rock hill. Other crews cleared the trees behind the fort and began to construct new houses. At this time of the year there are many deer in this region and there is good fishing out on Morris Reef all year long so food was not a worry. In a very short time both the fort and the houses were completed and the people were free to begin the blockade of Sitka.

THE BLOCKADE BEGINS

Anytime canoes were sighted heading toward Chaatlk'aanoow they were quickly intercepted and turned away with the warning, "Stay away from Sheet'ká! The Kiks.ádi remain at war with the Anooshee and will not allow trading canoes to pass Chaatlk'aanoow. Sheet'ká still belongs to the Kiks.ádi."

At first many canoes appeared and were turned away, but as time went by fewer and fewer canoes were sighted.

The blockade became even more effective once the Yankee traders learned of the blockade and sought to exploit it. They set up a trading station across from Chaatlk'aanoow on Catherine Island to the south. Even to this day it bears the name "Traders Bay." Trader canoes from all over the northern end of Southeast Alaska came to trade with the Yankee traders at Traders Bay.

THE SPECIAL ENVOY

Baranof sent many envoys to meet with the Sheet'ká Kiks.ádi as he attempted to break the blockade of Sitka. One such event is told by Cyrus Peck, Sr.: "The Russians could speak fluent Tlingit. When the Kiks.ádi blockade of Peril Straits began to hurt the Russian fur trade, Baranof sent a special envoy to Chief Katlian at Chaatlk'aanoow near Point Craven."

The special envoy was intercepted down by False Island by the Kiks.ádi canoes. The envoy said he had a special message from Baranof to War Chief Katlian. The Kiks.ádi canoes escorted him to Chaatlk'aanoow.

The envoy's canoe waited off shore to be greeted as he knew Tlingit custom required him to do. He waited and waited, but no one came forward to greet him, or to invite him ashore.

Chief Katlian refused to greet the envoy because he considered the envoy to be below his rank and station as War Chief of the Kiks.ádi people. He considered himself to be the equal of Baranof. So after a suitable delay he sent a messenger to tell the envoy, "You are below the rank of Katlian and he cannot greet you in person."

The envoy was deeply offended and loudly proclaimed his Russian and European nobility titles, but Katlian still refused to greet him.

After drifting offshore for a while longer the special envoy came ashore by himself. He walked over to the Chief Katlian's house and spoke in a loud voice, saying,

Oh, great Katlian!

Oh, great Katlian!

Mighty War Chief of the Sheet'ká Kiks.ádi people.

The Lord Baranof has dispatched me to carry his message to you, oh great chief Katlian.

Your life and your presence is like unto the sunshine!

Your life and your presence is like unto the sunshine!

Where you are, there is the bright sunshine!

Without you there is no sunshine!

Sheet'ká is now a land without sunshine!

Sheet'ká is now a land without sunshine!

The great Baranof sends you this personal message:

Oh, great Katlian!

Oh, great Katlian!

Return with your proud people to you ancient homeland.

Return to Sheet'ká.

Come home to Sheet'ká.

Let the sunshine return to Sheet'ká.

Let us live in peace!

Let peace return to our people!

Let us live in the sunshine!

Bring the sunshine back to Sheet'ká!

Bring your people back home to Sheet'ká!"

So says the great Baranof.

War Chief Katlian called a council meeting of the house chiefs and their shaman as required by tradition. One of the older chiefs spoke in favor of accepting the offer, but he was quickly shouted down by the younger chiefs who said, "The entire Tlingit nation will laugh at us if we return to Sheet'ká at the invitation of Anooshee. They will say we have surrendered and are now the willing slaves of the Anooshee! It is not the place of the Anooshee to invite the Sheet'ká Kiks.ádi back home to Sheet'ká. We will return when the time is right."

The shaman and the house chiefs voted to reject the offer.

Chief Katlian appointed one of his young nephews to deliver his message to the envoy.

As per his instructions the young nephew stopped some distance away from the special envoy and called in a loud voice:

The War Chief Katlian makes this reply:

The sun rises each morning in the east to bring warmth to the people and animals of this earth,

but each evening it sets in the west to mark the end of the day.

The Sun does not stay up in the sky forever.

There is a season for the moon.

There is a season for the stars.

For now the sun has set in Sheet'ká and it is the season of the moon and stars.

The sun will return to Sheet'ká when the time is right.

We await the proper time.

Let it be known that it is not the place of the Anooshee to invite the proud Kiks.ádi people to return to their ancient homeland. Sheet'ká still belongs to the Kiks.ádi. We will return to our ancient homeland when we say that the time is right. For now we will remain here in Chaatlk'aanoow. Chaatlk'aanoow has been good to us.

We will not leave Chaatlk'aanoow.

We will not end the blockade.

Now go!

Give War Chief Katlian's answer to your lord Baranof who lives in the land without sunshine.

The special envoy stepped back aboard his canoe and departed for Sitka.

Each year for many years Baranof sent special envoys to ask the Kiks.ádi to return home. Each time the Kiks.ádi refused.

One spring morning the Sheet'ká Kiks.ádi appeared outside of Nakwasina Sound near the "Beehive" and pulled their canoes ashore on the gravel beach just to the west of the Beehive and set up a new village camp.

A year or two later they landed back in Sheet'ká and immediately began to build their new winter quarters right up against the Russian stockade. They also announced to the Russians, "The mountains around Sitka belong to the Sheet'ká Kiks.ádi. No Russians will be allowed to hunt for deer or bear on those mountains while the Sheet'ká Kiks.ádi are here. Should any Russian or Aleut attempt to hunt on those hills they will do so at their own peril. When you need game you shall send a message to Chief Katlian who will assign hunters to go after the game.

"The hunters will exchange the game for Russian trade items."

The Sheet'ká Kiks.ádi had returned to their ancient homeland!

And so, as far as the Sheet'ká Kiks.ádi people are concerned, the Battle of Sitka of 1804 came to an end many, many years after the shooting stopped. It ended when their canoes again touched the beaches of Sheet'ká and they stepped ashore.

They did not know it then, but the Sitka Kiks.ádi people were to be the last of the Tlingit people ever to send its warriors into a full-scale battle against the white intruders from Europe.

No other Tlingit tribe or clan ever mounted such a defense of their homeland again.

The determined resistance of the Sitka Kiks.ádi helped stem the tide of Russian expansion in the Pacific Northwest. It forever changed the course of history in southeast Alaska.

However the Russians may have viewed the battle at that time and however history may view that battle today, at that time the Battle of Sitka of 1804 clearly showed the rest of the world that the Russian forces in Alaska were too weak to conquer the Tlingit people. It also showed them that the Tlingit people would fight to defend their homeland.

Today Baranof is long gone. Only a distant memory of him remains.

Lisianski and the *Neva* are gone.

The Anooshee roughnecks are gone.

The four hundred Aleut hunters are gone.

To this day the Sheet'ká Kiks.ádi people still live in their ancient homeland.

War Chief Katlian, Shaman Stoonookw, House Chief Skawu Yéil and all the other participants in this great battle are still recalled when the Sitka Kiks.ádi come together to celebrate the events in their lives.

The Kiks.ádi and the Kiks.ádi yatx'i are still a strong part of the Sheet'ká tribal structure.

But one thing has changed—Sheet'ká is now called "Sitka."

***

CLAN CONFERENCE PHOTOS

The First Conference of Tlingit Clans and Tribes
May 5 - 8, 1993
Klukwan/Haines, Alaska

PHOTOS BY PETER METCALFE

A panel discussion on the Tlingit language draws a comment by the late Matthew Fred of Angoon. To his immediate right are Walter Soboleff, Anna Katzeek and the late Elizabeth Nyman.

The late Judson Brown addresses conference participants. Paul Jackson (left) awaits his turn to welcome the guests.

82   Will the Time Ever Come?

Wolf Night, Friday, May 6, 1993 *From left to right: Kelly James, Jon DeWitt, the late Forrest DeWitt Jr., Tom Jimmie, Charlie DeWitt, Andy Hope, and Gerry Hope.*

Lydia George and her sister-in-law Margaret Abbott during the orientation session that opened the first Conference of Tlingit Tribes & Clans at Haines, Alaska, May 5, 1993.

Sergei Kan, Dartmouth College

The Chilkat River village of Klukwan, Alaska, 23 miles up the highway from Haines.

Gilbert Fred and Jan Criswell examine a bear hat at the Kaagwaantaan Bear House in Klukwan.

Totemic crests within the Killer Whale Dorsal Fin House (Dakláweidi Ligooshi Hít) at Klukwan.

Clan Conference participants visit the Kaagwaantaan Bear House in Klukwan. Joe Hotch (center) is the caretaker of the Bear House.

Clan Conference 87

Dancers, left to right facing camera: Ruth Willard, Ed Hotch, Jackie Johnson, Margaret Abbott. At right, back to camera, Bessie Fred.

Raven dancers led by Matthew Fred, left.

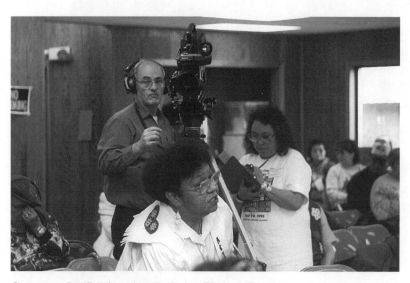
Cameraman Dan Etulain assisted by the late Elizabeth "Sister" Hope recording archival video of conference activities.

Clan Conference 89

Richard Jackson, right, leading the Tongass Tribe in dance.

Sam Johnson, Teslin, greets the crowd on Raven Night.

Joe Hotch, Klukwan, says farewell to conference participants on the last night. Left, seated, is the late Austin Hammond, Haines, and standing to Joe's left, Paul Jackson.

PART II

CONTEMPORARY ISSUES & PROJECTS

THE SOUNDS OF ENGLISH AND TLINGIT

BY RICHARD DAUENHAUER
SEALASKA HERITAGE FOUNDATION
JUNEAU, ALASKA

Language has a profound influence on culture and world view, and it is a tragedy of our age that Native American languages are in peril. Tlingit is no exception. Like other Native languages, Tlingit was traditionally an oral language, but it is one that will not survive unless it becomes a written language which is read. The popular writing system used today for Tlingit was developed fairly recently, beginning in the 1960s with the work of Constance Naish and Gillian Story and continuing with the work of Nora and Richard Dauenhauer and Jeff Leer in the 1970s through the present. Thanks to their efforts, we now have a rich Tlingit literature in the written word to supplement the oral traditions. But in order for people to access this wonderful literature they must come to terms with the standard Tlingit orthography that is being employed. Like popular systems of writing used for other Native American languages, the Tlingit orthography takes advantage of the English alphabet to represent Tlingit sounds, thus facilitating their mastery among learners for whom English is their dominant language. But as Richard Dauenhauer points out in this essay, popular orthographies can be deceptively simple. As the Tlingit sound chart shows, there are many sounds and combinations of sounds in Tlingit that we don't find in English. Mastery of these sounds requires more than just a knowledge of linguistics and orthography: it takes oral practice and a conscious effort to distinguish Tlingit sounds from those of English.

PREPARED FOR THE TLINGIT CLAN CONFERENCE
MAY 1993

94   Will the Time Ever Come?

In hearing and learning a new language, it is normal to replace the unfamiliar sounds of the new language with the familiar sounds of the language we already use. Therefore, it helps to know where the two languages are the same, and where they are different. As the accompanying charts show, the sounds of Tlingit are much more difficult than English, and Tlingit has many sounds that are not found in English. This makes it hard for speakers of English to hear and pronounce Tlingit. This also makes it very hard to figure out spellings of Tlingit names from old sources, such as the Russian records and early writers such as Emmons and others. The sound charts show where the points of difficulty lie. These are the places we need to be careful in learning Tlingit names and words from the elders.

Example 1. Gunalchéesh. The "Indian L" in the middle of this word is found in all Native languages of Alaska, but is not found in English. This sound is often dropped out, or changed to a similar sound in English or Tlingit, so that you may hear:

> Guna__chéesh
> Gunash-chéesh
> Gunas-chéesh
> Gunax-chéesh
> Gunax̱-chéesh

Example 2. Tláa. The TL sound never begins a word in English, but is very common in this position in Tlingit. It becomes KL

klaa	(tláa)
klane	(tlein)
Klinkit (Lingít; Tlingit)	

Example 3. Dleit. The DL sound never begins a word in English, but is very common in this position in Tlingit. It becomes GL

glate	(dleit)
glaa	(dlaa; tlaa)

As the charts show, the most difficult problem area is the many K and X sounds in Tlingit. Most of these merge with English K, sometimes H. Tlingit Xutsnoowú becomes English "Kootsnoowu" or "Hootsnoowu."

There are 16 "K" and "X" sounds in Tlingit, but only 1 in English. So, 15 of the Tlingit sounds are usually lost, and become "K" or "H" in English.

Example 4. Yátx'i. This word means "children," and is the plural of yádi, which means child. It is very common in songs. The X' usually becomes K.

> yátki   (yátx'i)

Example 5. All the K and X sounds are difficult for learners to distinguish. Thus, in learning songs or names, it is easy to confuse:

> ya<u>x</u>   like
> yax'   at the face of.

Both may become "yuck."

Many combinations of sounds are difficult to hear in Tlingit. For example, T and CH may come together, and BOTH be pronounced, unlike English. Combinations of unfamiliar sounds occur, such as words ending in -K<u>K</u>W.

Tlingit is not an easy language to learn. The sounds are very difficult, and often take years to hear and pronounce. There are about 30 sounds in Tlingit not found in English. But these charts may help by showing where the difficulties lie. Like nautical charts for boating, sound charts can show you where the dangers lie.

Four K and X Sounds

The basic four *k* and *x* sounds can also be rounded as well. Tlingit has one of the most complicated sound systems of any language in the world. The chart below shows why. Of the three features—**backing, rounding,** and **pinching**—a *k* or *x* sound may have one, two, or three in any combination.

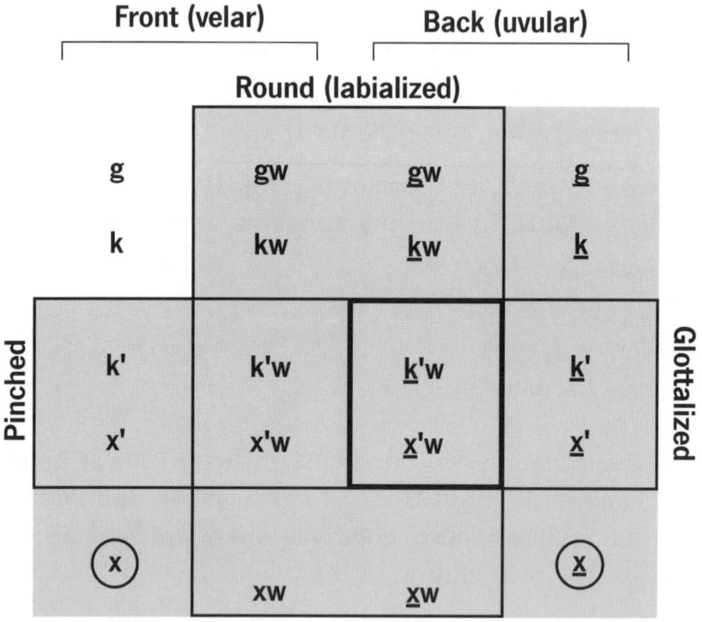

	Front (velar)		**Back (uvular)**	
		Round (labialized)		
g	gw	g̲w	g̲
k	kw	k̲w	k̲
k'	k'w	k̲'w	k̲'
x'	x'w	x̲'w	x̲'
(x)			(x̲)
	xw	x̲w	

(left side: Pinched; right side: Glottalized)

Of the twenty *k* and *x* sounds, eighteen are not shared with English. Shaded sounds are not shared with English; circled sounds are found in German. The bold lined box encloses the two Tlingit sounds (k̲'w and x̲'w) in which all three features—backing, pinching, rounding—are heard.

Technical Sound Chart

Unlike English

Like English in some places, but not in others. Still a problem.

◯ Found in German *ich* and *ach,* but not in English

		Dental	Aspirated	Glottalized ("pinched")	Aspirated	Glottalized	Nasal	Semivowels
Front of Mouth	Dental	d	t	t'			n	
	Lateral	dl	tl	tl'	l	l'		
	Alveolar	dz	ts	ts'	s	s'		
	Alveo Palatal	j	ch	ch'	sh			
	Velar	g	k	k'	(x)	x'		y
	Velar Rounded	gw	kw	k'w	xw	x'w		w
Back of Mouth	Uvular	g̲	k̲	k̲'	(x̲)	x̲'		
	Uvular Rounded	g̲w	k̲w	k̲'w	x̲w	x̲'w		
	Glottal	•			h			

Vowels

Short: a   i   e   u

Long: aa   ee   ei   oo

Tones

High: ´

Low: unmarked; formerly `

BUILDING A TLINGIT RESOURCE ATLAS

BY THOMAS F. THORNTON
ANTHROPOLOGY PROGRAM
UNIVERSITY OF ALASKA SOUTHEAST

Much is made of the close physical, social, and spiritual ties that the Tlingit and other indigenous peoples have to the natural world. This world view stems from the fact that Native peoples tend to imagine themselves as organic inhabitants of a community of beings, both human and non-human, which non-Natives often blithely simplify as "the environment." To understand and convey Tlingit views of and relationships to the natural world, Tom Thornton argues that it is necessary to probe Tlingit ethnogeography and cosmology at the deepest levels. This means answering basic questions, like what is the environment? A natural resource? A cultural resource? All of these terms are used and defined in various ways in the public policy arena, but Thornton asks, how do Tlingits define them? He advocates building a Tlingit resource atlas that illustrates Tlingit conceptions, an atlas which might, through the power of maps and visual iconography, help Natives and non-Natives alike to better understand the profound ties that Tlingits have to the lands and waters of Southeast Alaska.

What is a natural resource? What is a cultural resource? Historically, these concepts have been, by and large, narrowly conceived in environmental and social research. Natural resources have been almost exclusively defined on the basis of their potential for economic development, while inventories of cultural resources have focused mainly on the age and significance of physical remains, to the exclusion of non-material factors. Too often important resources that do not meet these criteria are ignored or undervalued in the planning process. Although planners have begun to consider other factors in assessing the environmental and social impacts of development, such as sacredness and aesthetics, the process remains annoyingly constrained by parochial conceptions and by state and federal priorities.

But what if the process of defining important natural and cultural resources was not thus constrained by public policy guidelines and deadlines? What if, moreover, the process was locally and culturally based? For example, how would Yakutat, or Klukwan, or Angoon Tlingits today identify, describe, and inventory their local natural and cultural resources? How would this compare to an inventory conducted by the Forest Service or other outside agencies? It seems clear that Tlingit communities would use a broader set of criteria in defining and valuing resources.

Is such a project worth doing? On the following pages I explore the viability of producing a Tlingit resource atlas based on a process where Native communities define, inventory, and record their resources using traditional and modern forms of representation. After highlighting the need for and benefits of the project, I will outline a general process through which the work might proceed and suggest some potential maps that might be included in the final product.

WHAT IS A TLINGIT RESOURCE ATLAS?

A Tlingit resource atlas is a book I wish existed but does not. Indeed, the notion of producing the atlas is born somewhat out of frustration. Frustration that there is not a good comprehensive guide to the Native history, occupancy, and use of Southeast Alaska, or other areas for that matter. Frustration that the concept of a resource is defined too narrowly in the public policy arena. Frustration that the documentary sources that should exist and which would improve the scope and minimize the impacts of planning do not exist, and have to be hastily compiled or too briefly summarized by researchers or agency personnel, from outside the affected communities. And frustration that the process by which the natural and cultural landscapes are now being managed and transformed (too often for the worse) is too centralized and removed from the places and people that are affected. I am sure that some of you have shared these frustrations, which tend to surface at public hearings, where the conflicts inherent in these issues often manifest themselves in heated debate. I'm not suggesting that a resource atlas will soothe all of these frustrations. If it was that easy, it would have been done long ago. However, a Tlingit resource atlas may help by refocusing the debate on the environment at the philosophical level. When I think about a culturally-based resource atlas, I'm thinking about a document that would challenge the dominant assumptions not only about what resources the environment contains, but what the landscape itself means; a document that would turn on its head the conventional, one-dimensional, or purely physical view of the landscape, by including representations of the landscape (including—but not limited to—maps, illustrations, and narrative) which portray the values and beliefs, pathways, and practices of those people who have occupied and used the land for so many centuries. In this part of the world that means Tlingits.

But at the risk of going off the metaphysical deep end, I will lay down some key concepts that I think are fundamental to the enterprise. Let's start with the term *landscape*. By *landscape* I am referring to the human orientation to the environment. While the natural environment is mainly conceived of as a physical thing, landscape itself is composed of at least three dimensions. These include:

1) tangible and physical features of an area, such as mountains and streams, that are regularly included in atlases, planning documents, and resource inventories;

2) measurable activities of humans, be they the harvest of salmon for subsistence or the commercial harvest of timber for pulp;

3) meanings and symbols that are imposed on the environment by human consciousness. It is this element, the symbolic

meaning, that enlivens the landscape, gives its emotive and spiritual power, and characterizes its representation in art and other spheres of human life.

Typically, it is not the business of atlases to deal with this third dimension. Yet to ignore the symbolic element is to accept the implicit assumption of the planner that the land is merely a conglomeration of physical resources, each of which can be valued in "real" dollars according to its economic potential. To ignore the symbolic is to rule out the possibility of linking landscape to beliefs, identities, and values—in short, to life itself.

I might draw the distinction another way by suggesting that an exploration of the symbolic allows us to understand not only what it means to use a place, but what it means to inhabit a place. This concept of inhabitation is fundamental to our understanding of indigenous peoples and much more profound than mere environmentalism. As the writer Wendell Berry explains it:

> The concept of country, homeland, dwelling place becomes simplified as "the environment"—that is, what surrounds us. Once we see our place, our part of the world, as surrounding us, we have already made a profound division between it and ourselves. We have given up the understanding—dropped it out of our language and so out of our thought—that we and our country create one another, depend on one another; that our land passes in and out of our bodies just as our bodies pass in and out of our land; that we and our land are part of one another, so all who are living as neighbors here, human and plant and animal, are part of one another, and so cannot possibly flourish alone; that, therefore, our culture must be our response to our place, our culture and our place are images of each other and inseparable from each other, and so neither can be better than the other.
>
> *(Berry 1977:22)*

It seems to me that today, as in the past, a lack of understanding on the part of the dominant culture—and here I am referring to big industry and national environmental organiza-

102   Will the Time Ever Come?

tions alike—of the concept of inhabitation has not only hurt
the interests of Native peoples, but also served to impoverish
the landscape for all of us. In proposing a culturally based resource atlas, I am advocating a publication that takes the themes
of inhabitation and all three dimensions of landscape seriously.

WHY AN ATLAS?

A Tlingit resource atlas which stresses inhabitation and successfully integrates the multiple dimensions of landscape has
the potential to revitalize our sense of the landscape and what
it means to inhabit one as opposed to simply utilize or preserve
one. In addition to these lofty philosophical motives, however,
I think there are some other practical reasons for producing a
Tlingit resource atlas. Specifically, the atlas would have both
scientific and educational applications.

SCIENTIFIC APPLICATIONS

Perhaps the most important scientific application would be
to fill in gaps in the literature. Much has been written about
the Tlingit and other Native American groups in anthropological circles and elsewhere, but remarkably little of the published
literature sheds a regional light on Southeast groups' relationships with specific landscapes and resources. One reason for
this is that such projects are a lot to bite off and probably more
than a single researcher can chew. Thus many choose to limit
themselves either geographically (to a single community) or
topically (to a particular resource, ritual, or other aspect of culture). Although important insights can be gleaned from such
texts, the narrow focus often separates the information from
the larger setting and from the landscape. Thus we find writers
waxing on about the carvings on halibut hooks without talking about fishing places, or analyzing totem poles without dis-
cussing social organization or property.

Such abstractions belie the importance of landscape and natural resources, not only in the context of traditional Tlingit culture, but in the context of contemporary society as well. To
slightly rephrase a popular campaign phrase from the 1992 elec-

tion, "It's the land stupid!" Of course there are exceptions to this pattern. Two outstanding studies of Tlingit culture that are attentive to landscape are Frederica de Laguna's published works on Yakutat (1972) and Angoon (1960). Another, which is not limited to a single community, is George Thornton Emmons' The Tlingit Indians. (Some of Emmons' other important unpublished work on the history of Tlingit tribes and clans can be found in the appendix of this book.) Emmons' regional approach and his experience and interactions with Tlingits from Cape Fox to Yakutat and inland create an interesting dynamic in his narrative: For although a book about "The" Tlingit Indians assumes a certain unity, as an inveterate traveler and careful observer, Emmons was often more struck by the differences between Tlingit groups than the similarities.

In addition to the general ethnological literature, there is the more specialized technical literature produced by government organizations, such as the Bureau of Land Management, the Forest Service, and the Alaska Department of Fish and Game (to name just a few) that play a role in resource management. These publications are always closely tied to land and resource issues and often feature a regional perspective. Many include extensive mapping and quantitative analysis along with ethnographic description. However, the scopes of various agencies' missions necessarily constrain them toward a preoccupation with those domains. For the Department of Fish and Game that means a tight focus on the harvest and use of fish and wildlife resources by Natives and non-Natives alike. Although we have detailed community maps showing historic and contemporary harvest areas for these species, left out are the plants, minerals, and, perhaps, other key elements of the landscape. Also lacking in many of these publications is any analysis of the symbolic dimension of landscape that I referred to above (while some of the academic literature, on the other hand, may be too concerned with symbolism). Even those of us who try to be attentive to the emotional, spiritual, and other non-material influences pertaining to land and resources in our writings, often find ourselves with little to go on.

This is where a Tlingit resource atlas could really help. It would have the potential not only to fill important gaps in the existing literature, but also to alter the way that research is done by making investigators more sensitive to values not normally considered in natural resource planning. Moreover, the atlas format, with its emphasis on spatial analysis, would make the information presented especially compelling and easy to reference.

EDUCATIONAL APPLICATIONS

By filling in gaps in the literature and adding to the knowledge base you are doing good science. But also consider the enormous educational value a Tlingit resource atlas would possess for both Tlingits and non-Tlingits.

Everybody knows how bad Americans are at geography. One remedy for our ignorance is to become more intimate with maps and atlases. Maps, with their ability to render a host of information and relationships in a single view, are a powerful teaching tool. I wonder how many Tlingit children could draw the traditional ḵwáan boundaries? Or identify which Southeast villages their clans inhabited? In fact, this information could be easily mapped in a Tlingit atlas in a way that would make it interesting to viewers.

HOW TO BUILD AN ATLAS

If a Tlingit atlas is good philosophy, good science, and good education (and, perhaps, good politics—but that's a separate discussion), how do we build one? We should start by recognizing that it is not an easy task. The term atlas, which comes from Greek mythology (Remember the guy who held up the world?), means "anyone bearing a great burden." Surely, some Atlases will be needed to help build the Tlingit resource atlas. Undoubtedly, it will be a shared burden between Natives and non-Natives, professionals and laymen, artists and scientists, the living and the deceased (whose memories and teachings endure).

Assembling the atlas should be a process controlled at the local level, according to traditional patterns of sovereignty, land use, and social organization. The methodology should be consistent enough such that results can be aggregated across communities and to the regional level. Minimal guidelines for carrying out the study should include the following:

1) *Gathering existing information.* A wealth of information already exists on Tlingit—Southeast Alaska landscape relations. Sources pertaining to this topic come from a variety of disciplines, including natural science, social science, humanities, and legal studies. Having surveyed a large number of these sources on the topic of Tlingit place names, I can state that a literature review is potentially a very large task. This part of the work should be done by people with experience and some background in research and knowledge of the Tlingit literature.

As examples of how existing information can contribute to the development of a Tlingit resource atlas, I would like to highlight just a couple of sources here. One is a report to the Commissioner of Indian Affairs entitled, "Possessory Rights of the Natives of Southeastern Alaska" by Goldschmidt and Haas (1946). The objective of this report was to determine what lands the Natives of Southeast Alaska had in their possession in 1946 that they similarly held or claimed in 1894. Visiting Southeast Native communities in 1946 (certain communities, such as Hydaburg and Klawock, were excluded because they were covered by other investigations), the researchers took testimony from local Native experts regarding their historical occupancy and use areas. Some of the statements were recorded in Tlingit and translated by Joseph Kahklen, Sr., an assistant to the project. As you can imagine, the testimony contains a wealth of information, including details about Tlingit place names, subsistence patterns, settlement sites, fish camps, and so on. The report also includes a set of maps, although they are of poor quality by today's standards. Nevertheless, the Goldschmidt and Haas report could serve as a point of departure for additional inquiry into cultural geography and the production of Tlingit resource atlases.

In addition to these regional sources, there are local gems as well. I have already mentioned de Laguna's well-known works

106   Will the Time Ever Come?

on Yakutat and Angoon. But I wonder how many of you are aware of a marvelous map of the Indian country above Haines that was done in 1869 by the geographer George Davidson and the Chilkat leader Kohklux' (K̲alák̲ch'?)in a unique cooperative effort. Davidson's mission was to map what to Americans had previously been *terra incognita,* namely that region under the St. Elias and Yakutat Ranges and the Yukon River extending down to Chilkat territory. In a wonderful exercise in cross-cultural communication, he engaged the Chilkat leader to work with paper and pencil for several days creating a map of this area. As Davidson tells it, the endeavor "cost him (Kohklux') and his two wives two or three days' labor with pencil and no rubber...It began at Point Seduction, in Lynn Canal, with islands, streams and lakes; and with mountains in profile (1901:76)." To this Kohklux' added information about distance (in terms of day's travel by foot), camping places, and geographic names. Needless to say, Davidson was quite impressed. For his part, Kohklux' was equally impressed with Davidson's ability to transcribe Tlingit sounds on paper such that he could read Tlingit place names back to the chief in his own tongue, and Kohklux' desired very much to learn how this was done. We are fortunate that this collaborative research was recorded and can be used by Chilkat Tlingits and other groups as a source of Tlingit place names, historic trails, trade routes, and other information that might be included in a resource atlas.[*]

These are just two examples of good sources that exist but may not be widely known. There are countless other sources pertaining to Tlingit resources that could be similarly referenced.

2) *Evaluating existing information.* Once material has been gleaned from the appropriate existing sources, it should be carefully reviewed and evaluated. Cross-cultural communication being what it is, there are undoubtedly errors and omissions in the existing literature. In some cases, information that was correctly recorded may have been incorrectly interpreted. It is im-

---

[*] An annotated version of Kohklux's map was published by the Yukon Historical & Museums Association under the title The Kohklux Map in1995.

Figure 1
Kohklux' Map

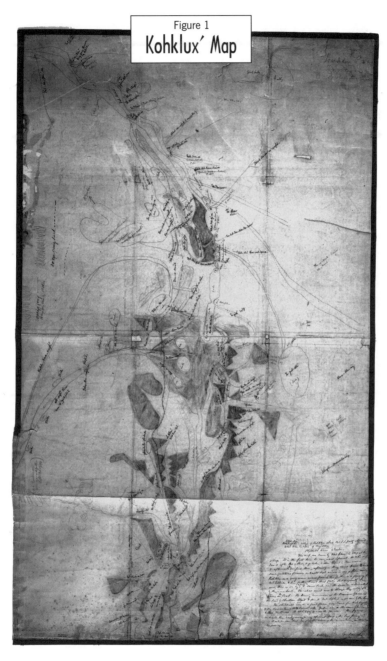

This map is a photograph of Kohklux's original drawn in 1869 for the geographer George Davidson. The map details dozens of travel routes, camping places, and other named sites. Courtesy of the Yukon Historical Society and the Bancroft Library, University of California, Berkeley.

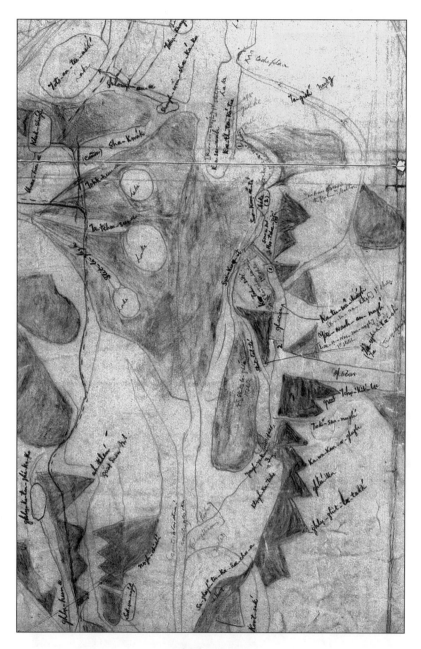

Kohklux' Map
(detail)

portant not to reproduce these errors, but rather to use the opportunity of a new publication to correct them. By evaluating existing information, community members will not only be educating and empowering themselves, but also serving the larger academic community by defining more clearly their history, geography, and culture. Hopefully, errors can be corrected in the process, and omissions can be remedied by devoting new research efforts toward filling the gaps.

3) *Soliciting new information.* After identifying deficiencies in the existing literature, Native communities could then turn to setting their own research agenda. Procedures and guidelines could be set up for carrying out the research. Although specific procedures and guidelines may vary according to the needs of each community, a uniform methodology should be adhered to so that results will be comparable.*

4) *Assembling the information into a meaningful whole.* This is perhaps the most exciting part. An important benefit of compiling a resource atlas is that it allows a community to assimilate and interpret a variety of disparate information and weave it into a new, more meaningful whole. Not only will each map or representation tell a story, but the whole publication will tell a story as well. With local control and cooperation with outside experts, a balance can be achieved such that the final product will be of use to many audiences and will remain a definitive source of information on natural and cultural resources for a long time to come.

5) *Funding.* One key ingredient that I have not addressed is funding. Obviously many of the above tasks will require financial support, which may be scarce. Here again, hopefully, cooperation can prevail and funding for the research and production of a Tlingit resource atlas can be a collaborative effort between local and regional and Native and non-Native organizations. In fact this is already going on in some areas. The Alaska

---

* For example, I have prepared a methodology for the collection and mapping of Tlingit place names. This methodology has since been applied in the Southeast Native Subsistence Commission's Native Place Name Project which has (as of 1997) worked in partnership with ten Tlingit communities to document more than 2300 Native place names.

Department of Fish and Game, Division of Subsistence, for example, has supported a research project on Tlingit geography and uses of Glacier Bay National Park that is being carried out jointly with the Huna Traditional Tribal Council. One outcome of this ongoing research has been a Tlingit place name map of Glacier Bay, a draft copy of which has been presented at this conference.* There also may be opportunities for completing research products under the auspices of other planning efforts that may be funded by outside agencies, such as the Coastal Zone Management Program. I was very pleased to see a Tlingit map of important named places in Mitchell, Hood, Chaik, and Whitewater bays produced as part of Angoon's Coastal Zone Management Plan. The place name maps were published in support of a recommendation to designate these valuable cultural resource areas as Areas Meriting Special Attention (AMSA), thus entitling them to special protections under the law (Angoon CZMP 1990).

POTENTIAL ATLAS INGREDIENTS

The proper business of atlases is to house maps, but they need not be limited to maps. Text, illustrations, and photographs could be key ingredients. I will focus here only on maps, which I have grouped under two categories: physical geography and ethnogeography.

I. PHYSICAL GEOGRAPHY

Physical geography is basic to any understanding of the landscape. Although there is a great deal of consistency in the physical geography of Southeast Alaska, we know that each area has its own peculiarities as well. Both similarities and differences with the regional landscape could be emphasized in this section of the atlas. Biophysical resource inventories and mapping have already been done for many Southeast villages in the context of Alaska Coastal Zone Management Program. Physical geography maps may include:

---

* See also Thornton (1995) for comparions of Tlingit and Euro-American place names in Glacier Bay.

1. Location of the Tlingit area
2. Land forms and topography
3. Geology
4. Glaciology
5. Hydrology
6. Ecology: including vegetation, fish and wildlife habitats, etc.

II. ETHNOGEOGRAPHY

Ethnogeography means adopting indigenous peoples' perspectives of the landscape and highlighting the cultural elements—such as language, social organization and property tenure, cosmology, economics, and history—that make Southeast Alaska a Tlingit landscape.

A. LINGUISTIC GEOGRAPHY

By linguistic geography, I am referring to Tlingit place names and to the boundaries of language groups and subgroups. With respect to place names, it is worth noting how much more descriptive of the geology, biology, hydrology, and history of Southeast Alaska history Tlingit place names are than their European and American counterparts, which are so often derived from European personal names (e.g., Baranof Island, Juneau). We also know that place names were basic to the fabric of social life. So it was that Kadashan, the great Wrangell leader, said to Governor Brady in 1898, "Ever since I have been a boy I have heard the names of different points, bays, islands, mountains, places where [Tlingits] get herring, [hunt] and make camps, that is why I think this country belongs to us" (Hinckley 1970:270). Linguistic geography maps might include:

1. Tlingit named places: a Tlingit gazetteer (see, for example, the 1995-97 maps produced by the Southeast Native Subsistence Commission Native Place Name Project);
2. Tlingit names for territories (ḵwáans) and neighboring peoples (see the list of Tlingit Tribes and Clans in the appendix of this volume);

3. Tlingit dialect boundaries (i.e., gulf coast, northern, southern, interior, and Tongass dialects).

B. SOCIAL GEOGRAPHY

Because social identities and patterns constrain interactions with lands and resources, social geography is also important to an understanding of the Tlingit landscape. As de Laguna (1960:17-18) suggested in her study of Angoon Tlingits, "It would be possible to show that the individual Tlingit's sense of history and geography is strongly affected by the dominance of the sib [or clan] which controls the social, political and ceremonial aspects of his life." Indeed, the clan or sib provides a kind of "unity" and "logic" to knowledge, the importance of which may exceed what de Laguna referred to as "a purely spatial and temporal framework." My own recent studies have confirmed this observation (Thornton 1997a, 1997b, 1999). The logic of Tlingit social geography could be represented by mapping such themes as:

1. Ḵwáan boundaries;
2. Ḵwáan and/or clan population figures in different periods;
3. clan and house distributions across Southeast Alaska;
4. important cultural sites related to particular social groups.

C. COSMOLOGY

A section of the atlas should be devoted to Tlingit cosmology, which has as its source Tlingit attitudes, feelings, and interpretations of the universe as a whole. Why is this important? It is important because the way we see and interpret the world influences how we act on the world. Since time immemorial, human societies have pondered and attempted to come to terms with the nature of the cosmos. A quick study of Tlingit myths and texts (e.g., Swanton 1909), indeed those of any Native American group, provides ample evidence of such theorizing. The motivation for doing this is more than plain curiosity—it reflects a deep-rooted need to have a stable and consistent basis into which to fit infor-

Clan Conference 113

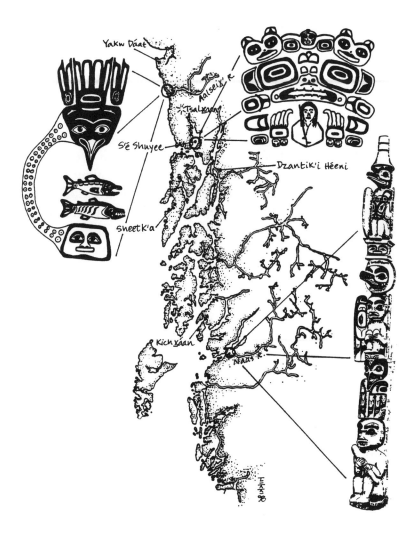

Figure 2

An example of a mythographic map incorporating various clan designs representing important stories and sites in their histories. Art by Nikki Morris incorporating Kiks.ádi, Chookaneidí, and L'uknax.ádi designs by Mike Jackson, Mary Johnson, and Robert Davis. Reproduced by permission.

mation about the known world, to extrapolate what unknown portions of it may be like, and to fit human existence into some form of universal order. This is as true of the New England Puritans as it is of the Northwest Coast Natives. And just as their cosmologies are vastly different, so too are their attitudes and interactions with the landscape.

The Raven cycle of stories, for example, provides a unique insight into Tlingit cosmology. Many of these stories show how specific elements of the universe, from daylight itself to particular land forms throughout the region, came into existence. Some of these events have been represented in artwork and other formats that could be included in the atlas along with the stories themselves. Unlike the other maps, which would be maps that tell stories, in this case the stories would "tell" the accompanying maps, so to speak. For instance, a group of stories might accompany a map showing regional land forms (mountains, streams, etc.) that were created by Raven.

Possible maps depicting important beliefs about the cosmos might include:

1. the geography of creation: including the creative deeds of Raven, etc.;
2. the geography of The Flood;
3. the geography of stars, planets, and other elements;
4. the geography of unseen or mythic landscapes.

Figure 2 is an example of a mythographic map that makes use of both Tlingit and western forms of representation.

D. HISTORY AND CULTURE

This is a wide open category that might include almost any set of spatial data deemed worthwhile by local communities. Also, it is likely to include the most sensitive topics, and therefore local organizations would need to be careful in screening what information they make available to the larger public. Potential maps under this category might include:

1. clan migration routes (e.g. Andy Hope's map in this volume);
2. Tlingit habitation and camp sites;
3. Tlingit trails and water routes; (e.g. the Kiks.ádi Survival March Trail);
4. fort and battle sites;
5. the geography of aboriginal villages (clan house locations, etc.);
6. the geography of clan houses (architectural design, carvings, crests, etc.).

E. ECONOMY

The section on economic geography should focus on both traditional and contemporary economic patterns, including both commercial and non-commercial activities. For example, a map detailing wood harvest areas could distinguish between traditional community harvest areas, Native regional and corporation logging areas, and other commercial timber harvests. Fishing maps might include not only historic subsistence areas, but commercial fish trap locations, and modern commercial fisheries. Fish and wildlife harvest maps have been completed recently for many Native communities in Southeast by Alaska Department of Fish and Game, Division of Subsistence. Similarly, maps showing historical logging may be available from the Forest Service. Possible maps in this section might include:

1. fishing areas and camps;
2. hunting areas and camps;
3. intertidal and upland gathering areas;
4. mineral resource areas;
5. wood or timber harvest areas;
6. trade routes;
7. the geography of industry and employment.

CONCLUSION

In concluding, I want to stress that what I have outlined here are simply some ideas for how to build a Tlingit resource atlas. I hope that we can explore these and other ideas in more detail in the future. If you are convinced of the worthiness of the concept, perhaps we can turn to issues of content and representation as well as the process by which the concept of a Tlingit resource atlas will become a reality.

References Cited

- ADF&G, Division of Subsistence and Huna Traditional Tribal Council. 1993. "Tlingit Place Names for the Glacier Bay Area, (Draft)." Juneau: Alaska Dept. of Fish & Game.
- Angoon Coastal Zone Management Plan. 1990. Final Approved Plan.
- Berry, Wendell. 1977. The Unsettling of America. New York: Avon.
- Davidson, George. 1901. "Explanation of an Indian Map...from the Chilkaht to the Yukon Drawn by Chilkaht Chief, Kohklux, in 1869." Mazama 2(2):75-82.
- de Laguna, Frederica. 1960. The Story of a Tlingit Community. Bureau of American Ethnology Bulletin 172. Washington D.C.: U.S. Government Printing Office.
- de Laguna, Frederica. 1972. Under Mount St. Elias: The History and Culture of the Yakutat Tlingit. Smithsonian Contributions to Anthropology. Washington, D.C.
- Emmons, George T. 1991. The Tlingit Indians. Frederica de Laguna, ed. Seattle: University of Washington Press and The American Museum of Natural History.
- Goldschmidt, Walter and Theodore Haas. 1946. "Possessory Rights of the Natives of Southeastern Alaska." Unpublished report. Washington D.C.: Commissioner of Indian Affairs. (Note: this report was edited and expanded, and published in 1998, under the title Haa Aaní, Our Land: Tlingit and Haida Land Rights and Use. Sealaska Heritage Foundation and University of Washington Press.)
- Hinckley, Ted C. 1970. "The Canoe Rocks Speak." The Western Historical Quarterly, July.
- Swanton, John R. 1909. Tlingit Myths and Texts. Bulletin 39. Bureau of American Ethnology. Washington, D.C.
- Thornton, Thomas F. 1994. "Methodology for Recording Tlingit Place Names." Southeast Native Subsistence Commission, Native Place Names Project, Guidelines and Procedures. Manuscript in the author's possession.
- Thornton, Thomas F. 1995. "Tlingit and Euro-American Toponymics in Glacier Bay." In Proceedings of the Second Glacier Bay Science Symposium, 1993. Anchorage, National Park Service.
- Thornton, Thomas F. 1997a. "Know Your Place: the Organization of Tlingit Geographic Knowledge." Ethnology 36(4): 295-307.
- Thornton, Thomas F. 1997b. "Anthropological Studies of Native American Place Naming." American Indian Quarterly 21(2): 209-228.
- Thornton, Thomas F. 1999. "What's in a Name? Indigenous Place Names in Southeast Alaska." Arctic Research of the United States 13(Spring/Summer): 40-48.

SUBSISTENCE AND CONTEMPORARY TLINGIT CULTURE

BY STEVE J. LANGDON
DEPARTMENT OF ANTHROPOLOGY
UNIVERSITY OF ALASKA ANCHORAGE

"You are what you eat" may seem like a trite cliché, but Steve Langdon shows why it is not for the Tlingit. Subsistence traditions among Alaska Natives are the basis not only for sustenance but also help to maintain the physical, mental, and sociocultural health of communities in a myriad of other ways. In addition, subsistence traditions are closely linked to historical settlements and migrations, and to the structure of Tlingit social organization and leadership. The continuing erosion of subsistence resource bases, rights, and traditions through Euro-American encroachment has had a variety of ill effects. Yet, a strong subsistence orientation remains a foundation of Tlingit culture—one Langdon argues is very much worth fighting for.

The Tlingit people have traditions of resource use and relationships with the land and sea in Southeast Alaska that go back hundreds and, in some cases, thousands of years. These ties have been fundamental in providing people with the food, clothing and other resources necessary to survive. They have also been fundamental to the cultural expressions and heritage of the Tlingit people. As the Tlingit people look to the 21st century, the relationships with the traditional resources of the region can and should continue to be a foundation of Tlingit cultural heritage and identity.

There are many reasons to aggressively support the continuation and enhancement of these activities, but there are also substantial threats to that continuity. In this brief overview, I will address aspects of the strength which use of traditional resources holds for the continuity of Tlingit cultural heritage and also note some of the threats to that use as well as the means to confront those threats.

TLINGIT SUBSISTENCE: TRADITIONAL

In traditional Tlingit society, many "property" or use rights were held to certain resource harvest locations by clan and house groups. Clan and house heads exercised trusteeship over these sites managing harvests from them by organizing labor and handling requests for use of the area by other Tlingit groups. Locations such as salmon streams, locations on rivers, shellfish beaches, berry patches, cedar trees and others were held, used and managed through this system. A summary of these practices and territories for Tlingit kwaans, except the Kake and Henya/Klawock people, was published in 1946 entitled *The Possessory Rights of the Tlingit Indians of Southeast Alaska*. Although useful, more information could be collected on these topics, especially from the groups not included, namely, Kake, Klawock/Henya, and Hydaburg. There are other sources of information, such as a systematic compilation of Tlingit place names, which Jeff Lear of the Alaska Native Language Center and Tom Thornton of the Subsistence Division of the Alaska Department of Fish and Game have begun to collect. The old, new and previously overlooked information should be integrated and republished with new, better quality maps.

It is possible that information on Kake and Klawock/Henya territories and clan uses are located in BIA archives associated with the establishment of reservations for these communities in the mid-1940s. Some materials may also be in Sealaska documents pertaining to the selection of Historic Sites under ANCSA. Wherever located, these materials need to be obtained and combined with others in the new publication.

The document should be used in the education of the youth as they are taught about traditional resources, their locations and methods of harvest, processing and consumption. Perhaps special materials will have to be developed for use among grade school children.

In addition to the information on locations and property rights, there are also substantial remains of ancient fishing structures found along the shores of Southeast Alaska. Surveys of the western Prince of Wales Archipelago has revealed over 25 locations with the remains of stone fish traps in the intertidal zone. Some of these, such as those at Naukati Creek and near Arrecife Reef, are in good condition and would be useful in demonstrating to the youth traditional capture methods. Other stone traps are exceptional for their scale or the underlying knowledge of salmon behavior on which their use is premised. Examples of these exceptional structures include Fern Point on San Fernando Island west of Craig and on the northshore of Naukati Bay where substantial schools of salmon bound for many creeks were intercepted prior to their entry into estuaries and streams.

Besides the intertidal stone traps, recent research has also identified the remains of wooden stake traps at the mouths of many streams. For example, stake remnants were found in the intertidal zone at the mouth of the Klawock River dating back to over 1,350 years ago. Continuing research at Little Salt Lake north of Klawock has identified an extraordinarily complex system of weirs which are now buried beneath the intertidal mud. Some of the stakes extend back up into the grassy flats indicating an earlier period of use. Although these structures have not been completely understood, their scale and complexity is easily demonstrated to young people and will instill a sense of pride and wonder in the accomplishments of their ancestors.

Another aspect of traditional subsistence practice that it might be useful to re-examine is the issue of trusteeship over resources. The importance of the trustee concept (as opposed to ownership) in traditional Tlingit society had two dimensions.

The first of these was that the house or clan leader was responsible for the welfare of the people of his clan or house group. That welfare extended to the physical, social and spiritual well-being of his people. The leader was also responsible for maintaining the resources over which he was the trustee and which were the source of the sustenance for his people. Tlingit people recognized the authority of trustees over resources and knew that in order to use a particular resource they must obtain the approval of the resource trustee.

Tlingit leaders sought to maintain their control following the coming of American salteries and canneries in the 1870s and 1880s, and in several cases their claims were recognized by Americans who paid fees to the Tlingit leaders for access to their resources. But in most cases this did not occur and by the 1890s, with larger numbers and military support, the American cannerymen ceased their recognition of Tlingit claims.

It can be interpreted that the cultural knowledge about harvest timing, escapements, ritual welcome, and many other aspects of the fishery accumulated and passed on through generations of Tlingit leaders was jettisoned through this change of jurisdiction. The upshot was the devastation of the sockeye resources of Southeast Alaska as the American canneryman sought merely short-term financial profit and lacked the sense of both human and resource trusteeship which their Tlingit predecessors held. As U.S. Fisheries Agent Jefferson Moser commented in 1899:

Whenever the 'Albatross' anchored near any locality permanently or temporarily inhabited by Natives, a delegation of the older men or chiefs came on board and requested an audience... At Klinkwan, Chacon, Klakas, Klawak, Metlakatla, Kasaan, Karta Bay, and, in fact, everywhere, the Indians were greatly exercised over their condition... These streams, under their own administration, for centuries have belonged to certain families or clans settled in the vicinity, and their rights in these streams have never been infringed upon until the advent of the whites. No Indians would fish in a stream not their own except by invitation, and they cannot understand how those of a higher civilization should be— as they regard it less honorable than their own savage kind. They claim the white man is crowding them from their houses, robbing them of their ancestral rights, taking away their fish by shiploads; that the Indians will have no supply to maintain himself and family, and that starvation must follow.

The elders clearly perceived the damage to the fisheries that the American cannerymen were perpetrating and objected as best they could. Unfortunately, the disappearance of the institution of trusteeship has resulted in damage to virtually all of the customary and traditional resources used by the Tlingit people. It may have also damaged the ethic of resource trusteeship.

Local trustees should be reinstituted to look after the resource for the benefit of the local people. The erosion of local authority over fish and game resources has made it difficult for people to visualize themselves as responsible for the resources now. In addition, the concentration of the population in larger settlements has made it harder to maintain vigilance on resources at a distance. A new ethic and foundation for local control over and benefit from resources requires a collective resurgence of interest and concern. Without it, the pattern of continuing external control and benefit of the fisheries of Southeast Alaska will continue.

TLINGIT SUBSISTENCE: CONTEMPORARY

The conduct of subsistence requires physical and mental exertion which helps to maintain a healthy human being. Being active in nature can provide a natural "workout" and creates an opportunity to free the mind and body from the lethargy of watching TV or playing Bingo. It creates value through active engagement of the individual in what they are doing. One of the benefits of traditional life is outdoor activity which will surely enhance both the physical and mental health of contemporary people.

The pervasive influence of media and consumerism often dulls people's sense of wonder and purpose that comes from interacting with nature. This is especially true of young people. Although it is often necessary to force youngsters and adolescents to undertake subsistence, in the long run it will be to their benefit, perhaps more so than anything else parents or grandparents can provide. I have seen many adults take pride in putting up fish, berries or deer and in the passing of those skills on to their children. Realizing the value of those activities often doesn't come until mid-adulthood when they have children and then the seed of subsistence planted in their youth takes root and grows to provide a vital new sense of self-worth. Donawáak (Austin Hammond) understood this well and sought to provide this experience to young people at his camp on the Chilkoot River. He had the right idea.

Subsistence activities create foods which provide good nutrition and diets if eaten in appropriate ways. Salmon, halibut, fish eggs, deer, greens, berries and the other wonderful foods can be embellished with modern spices and vegetables to create an extraordinary cuisine. Fresh foods are now widely regarded as the best foods for our health. By combining the foods with the activity, subsistence is a healthy way of life.

Traditional subsistence activities, and most contemporary ones, require the efforts of many. Groups were and are needed to adequately harvest and process most foods, especially salmon, the mainstay of the subsistence diet. This fact establishes a social context for connecting to others in a positive fashion. The coordination of effort towards a mutual goal, successfully carried out, creates a tremendous feeling of harmony and togetherness. One hears a great deal in the contemporary press about the decline of the family and the importance of instilling the young with family values. Subsistence activities represent a natural occasion for the expression of those values and for young people and older people to work together in accomplishing something meaningful.

Being a social occasion, subsistence activities also present the opportunity for transmission of cultural knowledge and values from elders to young people. Appropriate attitudes of respect and trusteeship, of giving, and the technical aspects of doing things correctly and efficiently can all be taught while working together. It is the way things have always been and should continue to be.

Finally, subsistence is important to the spiritual sense of Tlingit people whether they are now Christian or prefer traditional spiritual concepts. By spiritual I refer to the act of giving which links a person to others and provides an extraordinary bond as well as sense of self-worth. On many occasions I have seen young people return from beach seining, fish egg collecting or deer hunting with the fruits of their labor. I have watched as they divided up the share and then taken some to their grandparents or other elderly or indigent people in the community. It has seemed to me that more than thrill and esteem comes from the harvest; it is the spiritual bond of the gift-giver to the gift-recipient that seems to provide the greatest sense of self-worth to these young people. It is that joy that is so important to them.

Subsistence can feed other dimensions of the spirit. In the respect for nature's wonders - the ocean, sky, fish, birds and animals—both Christian and traditionalist can share even though their experiences might be somewhat different.

SUBSISTENCE: WORTH FIGHTING FOR?

I have tried to show how subsistence is important to a sense of identity as well its many other physical, nutritional, social and spiritual benefits. For all of these reasons, I believe that it is important for the Tlingit people to persist in these activities. Although sometimes it appears that state and federal governments have created impenetrable barriers to its practice, the real solution is to just do it. The benefits and feelings of self-worth will be worth the effort.

NAMING IN THE YEAR 2000

BY ELLEN HOPE HAYS

Clan name: Káakaltin, Raven Looking Forward
Clan: Kiks.ádi
Clan House: X'aaká Hit, Point House
Child of Kaagwaantaan: Andrew P. Hope, Ḵaushti

I am in the third generation of converted Christianized/Westernized Tlingit. I am monolingual, speaking one language, which I try to use with respect: English.

I know some endearing words and expressions used fondly by my grandparents and easily by my parents' generation. I use those words and expressions rarely. I am, for the most part, removed from them.

My maternal grandmothers were: Lottie Sloan Howard, Jenny Willard, Mary Sloan Simpson, and Amelia Sloan Cameron.

Paternal grandmothers: Mary Williams (Hope), who died at a young age, Mrs. Billy Williams, Mrs. Charlie Smith, and Mrs. Gus Klaney.

1799-1890s
Sitka was the seat of change in government, belief and practice, and in the all important business of trade.

Change from tribal living to Christianized/Westernized living was dramatically portrayed by life in the "Cottages" as they were commonly called in the times of our grandparents. Students coming out of Sitka Industrial Training School (now

Sheldon Jackson College) were given lots of help in constructing cottages. You will note that these were individual homes and not tribal clan houses. Some of the first families in the cottages were: John Newell, Ralph Young, Mr. Cook, George Howard, Peter Simpson, John Willard, Mrs. Amelia James (who later became Mrs. Don Cameron). You will recognize some of the Alaska Native Brotherhood founders' names. The cottages or cottage settlement was the place important to the founding of that organization.

1914-1950s

Our family was not raised (therefore) in the Tlingit traditional social system. If anything, only on the fringe of it. For us and many other Tlingit that we knew, this is the way it was.

We experienced lives of change, largely away from being tribal. Our parents' generation knew the initial impact of leaving behind what Grandma referred to as "Old Custom," now unacceptable and disallowed. "Onward Christian Soldiers" was the new battle song. Grandma spoke English, sang hymns, practiced a Christian life. The tribal ways were there but not really definable.

For most of my life, I was devoted to life in the Church. It was my choice. It was satisfying and meaningful.

I began to be a contemporary Indian in 1966. I joined the most beloved organization, the Alaska Native Brotherhood. I was a new wave young lady, ready, and personally aggressive, to participate in Native issues.

Since then I have been involved in learning Tlingit ways of the past and totally involved with contemporary tribal events and activities.

The thoughts that I want to share at this conference are on the subject of tribal naming in the year 2000. Soon.

HOW WAS NAMING DONE?

During the period of migration to settle, the people moved from the mainland down the several rivers. Those places were along the Inside Passage.

They moved with keen awareness of life around them, natural life in this maritime and tidal culture, and of other people. To find the right place to settle meant life or death. They communicated with nature, listening for all sounds and looking for sights that would offer direction.

These encounters and characteristics were important to remember and to claim ownership through naming. All of this momentum waned and lost its life when old customs weakened and the new culture grew strong.

In the case of my clan, the Kiks.ádi, the Frog was there to talk to them, to sing to them.

My dad translated my name this way: "Raven Looking Forward" and my daughter's name "Installment Plan." Where it is possible, it would be helpful and useful to translate the sound of the names to its thought or meaning: the interpretation of the name.

Names were given as a way of remembering happenings and the reasons for taking action. Songs were composed to express feelings about it. This basically did not continue past the 1820s. As far as I know, there are no names given to remember the battles we staged to resist the aliens, the white man; no names given to remember the devastation of fatal diseases which irreparably fractured our ancient order; no names given to bid farewell to "Old Custom"; no names given when clan-house-living saw its end; no names given to herald the Brotherhood and Sisterhood; no names given when we won our land claims suit in 1968; no new ballad to sing about our feelings/emotions/conflict; no new naming for the events in tribal happenings called ANCSA; no new names to proclaim how we came full circle and it was now OK to be Indian; no new names to put value on our very significant life happenings of the last twenty-five years.

Let's do it!

Our forebears related to such events through naming. Not only do we bring along the clan bank of names remaining, but we add to it for our children through future name giving.

I am,
Raven Looking Forward to naming in the year 2000.

PART III

APPENDIX

A. EXCERPTS FROM GEORGE THORNTON EMMONS "THE HISTORY OF TLINGIT TRIBES AND CLANS"

Letter from Frederica de Laguna	129
Taanta Kwáan, George Emmons manuscript	131
T'aaku Kwáan, George Emmons manuscript	138
L'uknax.ádi, George Emmons manuscript	142
X'at'ka.aayí, George Emmons manuscript	144
Sik'nax.ádi, George Emmons manuscript	145

B. TLINGIT TRIBES AND CLAN HOUSES   148

A. EXCERPTS FROM EMMONS

TRANSCRIBED BY ANDY HOPE

The excerpts from "The History of Tlingit Tribes and Clans" that follow are reprinted with the permission of the American Museum of Natural History. They have been edited only to update spellings in accord with modern Tlingit orthography and to eliminate minor infelicities. The publication of the complete History remains a work in progress. In a letter to the Juneau Empire (October 16, 1992), distinguished anthropologist Frederica de Laguna, who edited Emmons' other monumental work on the Tlingit, The Tlingit Indians (*American Museum of Natural History and University of Washington Press, 1991) explains why these excerpts were not published.

Dear Sir:

In an article title "Tlingit Journal: Manuscript to be key element of clan conference" which appeared in the Wednesday, September 23 (page 10) issue of the Juneau Empire, Andrew Hope took me to task for not having included in my edition of Emmon's great work The Tlingit Indians, the latter's manuscript, "The History of Tlingit Clans and Tribes." Mr. Hope called it "the guts of the manuscript" that I prepared for publication by the University of Washington Press in 1991. He finds it inexplicable that I should have omitted the "History," adding correctly that "an understanding of Tlingit clan relations" is essential for "a true appreciation of the Tlingit."

Before answering this criticism, let me first congratulate my friend Andrew Hope on his splendid program of a clan conference for all the "Tlingit style" tribes in Alaska and adjacent Yukon Territory and British Columbia. The working sessions at this conference should do much to clarify the fundamental principles of Alaskan clan organization and to reaffirm the values on which Native societies are based. I am particularly pleased that Andrew Hope found my help useful in securing a copy of Emmon's manuscript "History of Tlingit Clans and Tribes," on which the Tlingit delegates to the conference can build. My best wishes go for their success!

130 Will the Time Ever Come?

Emmon's "History" was not originally part of his monograph. It was written as a separate book, and finished in 1916, while he did not really get down to writing this great monograph until goaded by Dr. Goddard of the American Museum in 1924, although he had been collecting information and arranging his quantities of notes for years. It was only in his old age that he tried to insert the "History" into a chapter of the monograph. Because the "History" manuscript wasn't intended to be part of the book, it did not fit and its 200 pages would have increased <u>The Tlingit Indians</u> to an unmanageable size.

The real difficulty with the History manuscript is that it needs to be checked. The many places mentioned should be accurately located and their native names verified, something which can only be done in the field... I therefore felt it would be wrong to publish such an important manuscript with these inaccuracies. It is to be hoped that the Tlingit clan representatives to the Conference in April 1993 will be able to supply the information so badly needed. It should be noted that this work does not form one history, but consists of the separate histories of the clans... (W)hy I deferred the History to a later publication, I should evidently have given a fuller explanation.

Sincerely,

Frederica de Laguna

Professor Emeritus of Anthropology

Bryn Mawr College

Thus, Emmons' manuscript must still be considered a work in progress. As Dr. de Laguna anticipated, the subsequent Clan Conferences have added to our understanding of the Tlingit language, the proper names of individuals, and place names. After consultation, we decided to publish the following excerpts as a means of bringing it to a broader audience and sharing some of the wealth of valuable information it contains. Please note that question marks and bracketed words and phrases indicate editors' additions to, or uncertainties about, the Emmons' manuscript.

TAANTA KWÁAN

Taanta Kwáan (Sea lion tribe) take their name from their old home, the Prince of Wales Islands, which was called Taan (Sea lion) from the abundance of this animal on the rocky west and south shores. The name in more general use is Taangaash or Tongass. They constitute the southernmost of the Tlingit tribes and from their geographic position may be considered one of the [oldest, if] not the oldest, of the Tlingit tribes that originally occupied the Tsimshian peninsula, the Alaska borderland and contiguous islands. Our only information of this country is contained in the myths and legends of the creation, connected with the Nass river valley, which antedate the Tsimshian occupation, and the oldest and most important of the Northern Tlingit have family stories of a migration from this region. From early authentic sources there is little history of this people as their territory lay just between the Russian and the English occupation and was not on the route of trading vessels, and through disastrous wars and epidemics they formed but an inconsiderable body at the time of the American acquisition of Alaska.

Originally, they occupied an extensive territory including the southern half of the Prince of Wales Island, Annette Island extending to Dixon Entrance, the islands and shores about the entrance of Portland Canal and much of Behm Canal, and claim to have extended down along the Tsimshian littoral to the mouth of the Skeena. Early in the eighteenth century, after a period of disastrous warfare with the Haida of Masset, they were dispossessed from Prince of Wales Island when they crossed over to Annette Island, settling at Port Chester and at Tamgass Bay. Here they were attacked by the Stikine and the villages destroyed. They removed to Ka-dock-ku [?], generally known as Tongass, at the entrance of Portland Canal. Smallpox ravaged the coast from 1836-39, and fully a third of their number was carried off.

Upon our taking possession of Alaska, a military post, Fort Tongass, was established in 1868, near Ka-dock-ku [?] on

Tongass Island, but was abandoned in 1870. With the growth
of the white settlement at Ketchikan and the abandonment of
the salmon cannery on Prince of Wales Island, this old village
was deserted and the whole tribe, scarcely over a hundred in
number, scattered among the different white towns, but lived
principally at Ketchikan, though some settled at Metlakatla and
others at Wrangell:

WOLF FAMILIES	RAVEN FAMILIES
Teikweidí	Gaanax.ádi
Dakl'aweidí	

Of the three families that constitute this tribe the origin of
the two oldest is a matter of conjecture, and it seems most reasonable, from their traditions, that they were among the first of
the migrating bands to descend the Skeena and the Nass and
settle on the nearby coast, but there is a curious belief preva-
lent among the older people that one of these families, the
Teikweidí, came from over the sea. As told to me by a very
intelligent older man, the Teikweidí came from the ocean and
were the first people to reach the outer coast. They settled on
Dall Island off the southwestern portion of Prince of Wales Island. In time, they increased and were joined by people from
the Interior who had come to the coast and this combination
formed a nucleus from which the Tlingit, Haida and some
Tsimshian here derived.

There were two [sisters] originally, [who] represented two
parties; the elder remained hereabouts and took [residence] and
constituted the Tlingit. The younger crossed over to the Queen
Charlotte Islands and formed the Haida, who were known as
[nitch town na ha] (Something very old in a living thing man
or animal). The name Teikweidí followed as that of a family. In
confirmation of this relationship existing between the two
people, it is said that at death feasts, when the descendants of
the two branches meet, that the Tlingit were given the first
place in acknowledgement of age.

This claim [provides a] speculation field of much interest
when considered in relation to certain facts connected with the
possibility of a strain of ancient blood in these people. That the

shores of Dixon Entrance and the nearby coast, the home of the Tlingit, Haida and Tsimshian, is the center of Native intelligence and art is an acknowledged fact. Going in any direction from this region, that the neighboring people are much inferior is very evident. The question naturally arises as to the reason for this difference and to what means or influence is it attributable? It seems more than certain that the southwest coast from the Straits of Juan de Fuca to Cook Inlet has been peopled from the Interior, the rivers breaking through the barrier of Coast Mountains were the highways of travel. That the Tlingit have reached the coast in this way is told in most of the family traditions. [Even] those who claim a southern home about the Tsimshian coast refer in song and story to the Upper Nass and Skeena, but association with or knowledge of the Athapascans and other Interior people fails to find any evidence of either of the characteristics mentioned. We are continually confronted with the problem as to how these qualities were developed in so short a period, for these three people have not lived here so very long.

Considering the Pacific currents, there is an ocean current, the Kora Kora (black water) that in a steady flow runs east from Japan along the Aleutian Islands through the Gulf of Alaska and along the continental shore to California where it turns oceanward. It approaches the coast more closely at Dixon Entrance where the Queen Charlotte Islands stand out to meet, in consequence of which, drift material from the Asiatic shore is often stranded here. This leads to an article by Horace Davis, "On the likelihood of an admixture of Japanese blood on our Northwest Coast," published in the proceedings of the American Antiquarian Society 1870-72, in which he gives the following data concerning wrecks of Japanese vessels that through stress of weather and loss of propelling power have been carried by this stream to our shores.

1815- Junk adrift boarded at sea Lat. 32 degrees 45' N. Long.
166 degrees 57' W.
1819- Junk adrift seen about Lat. 49 degrees N. Long.
131 degrees W.

1830- Junk stranded at Point Adams
1833- Junk stranded off Cape Flattery, Wash.
1805- Junk stranded near Sitka, Alaska
1882- Junk stranded on the Aleutian Islands
1882- Junk stranded on Attu, Aleutians
1871- Junk stranded on Adak, Aleutians

In January 1916 a Japanese fishing boat caught off the harbor of Shinoda, Japan in a storm in which her main mast and rudder were carried away, drifted helplessly for twenty-four days across the Pacific and finally landed about Dixon Entrance.

While none of these incidents confirm the Native theory that some of the early settlers at this point were oriental, yet from subsequent events it shows how reasonably this might have occurred, and how a center of Asiatic culture might account for much that is problematical today.

The present families of this tribe represent only a part of those who claim to have lived here in the past and are now found scattered through the northern divisions. They have had many misfortunes, and through war, disease, and emigration they remain only a scattered few living in poverty about the different white settlements and camps.

The Teiḵweidí (Brown Bear rock house or cave people) are unquestionably the oldest family here. Their origin is unknown, but a close relationship with the Haida is recognized. The claim to an oriental descent has been mentioned. Some claim that they first lived on the Tsimshian coast and were driven out by the Tsimshian when, crossing Portland Canal, they settled on the mainland coast and adjacent islands, but, attacked by the Stikine, they were again forced to move to the southern shore of the Prince of Wales Island. They constituted the principal opponents of the Masset Haida in the conflict that drove them out of this locality and back again to the coast and islands, while others migrated northward. Their relationship with the Haida and Tsimshian is shown by the custom of erecting heraldic and mortuary columns wherever they have settled, but unlike the former people who place them in contact with the house, the doorway passing through the base, they place them in front or at the side of their dwellings.

The Da̱kl'aweidí are of Athabascan stock and, reaching the coast by way of the Stikine, came south and were the latest addition to this tribe. They have never held the same social position as the Tei̱kweidí, although they were more numerous in earlier days.

The G̲aana̱x.ádi claim to have descended the Nass or Skeena in very early days and later crossed over to the Prince of Wales Island and lived in all of the villages of this tribe and later about Klawock, on the central west coast of the island, at which point their principal family traditions were enacted. At some early period they settled at Port Stewart, just within the northern shore of Behm Canal, from which place Gaana̱x (Safe or sheltered) they took their name. In their northern migrations they must have migrated northward several times and extending from a very early to a later period, as is proved by those who are found among the Hoonah and Chilkat and were the original settlers [of] the Taku branch. The L'ukna̱x.ádi claim to have come from or to have been closely connected with this family in early days [and] to have formed a family of this tribe.

The earliest village[s] of which we have any record were those on the Prince of Wales Island that were taken by the Haida, who settled in them and retained their Tlingit names.

Suk̲kwáan (Grass town) was some fifteen miles north of Howkan, on the channel connecting with Bucareli Bay, the_____ shows the village as occupied by the Haida in 1888.

Klink̲wáan (Country of abundance of food), so named on account of the extensive exposure of beach at low water where shellfish and other seafood could be gathered with little exertion, was on a small island in Cordora Bay and was occupied in 1888.

Howkan (Behind the rock), near the southern entrance of Kaigani narrows, is the principal village of the Haida today.

Kaigani (Man's noise town) was an old summer village on the eastern shore of Dall Island, long since deserted.

Hetta, on the inland channels, north of Howkan, is said to have been a village and, confirmation of this, the petroglyphs hereabouts are said to have been made by the early residents.

After their expulsion from this country they crossed over to Port Chester, on Annette Island and lived at Taakw.aaní (Winter town) where the present Metlakatla stands. In this connection it may be said that they were spoken of locally as Taakwaneidi. In the first half of the 18th century they were defeated in an attack by the Stikine and the villages destroyed. This must have been an extensive settlement as shown by the clearing and the remains of houses and charred columns as late as 1884 when the Tsimshians from Old Metlakatla came here and built their present village. The Dakl'aweidí alone claim to have had eight houses here. Of those who survived, some crossed the island and settled in Tamgass Harbor at Ch'eix' áani (Thimble berry town) but again they were attacked by the Stikine. They had an old village, Ta see nuck (in the midst of pebbles) [possibly Sáasaxakw, "Place with sand beaches around it"] on Village Island across from Cat Island. Here smallpox decimated them, but as late as 1888 few of the Teikweidí and Gaanax.ádi remained but the lack of water compelled them to leave and go to Tongass. The principal living place in the last century was on Tongass Island at the entrance of Portland Canal named Kadúkuxuka (Cottonwood Island) from the growth of this tree on the island. In 1889 it consisted of twenty-four old communal houses with an equal number of totem poles; of the former eighteen were Teikweidí, five Dakl'aweidi and one Gaanax.ádi. Captain Mead of the U.S. Navy, in sailing here on 1888, estimated the population at 300, but in 1889 they numbered about 150, and about this time the whole village of Ketchikan (Under the eagle's wing) had become a center of trade and activity. At this time the people were generally leaving the old village and about the mouth of the creek were building small houses which became their permanent houses and [where] the greater number that survive are found today[.] Within this time two totem poles have been erected, the principal one in front of the house of chief of the Gaanax.ádi. Khart kuk' kuawat see [?] "Yeil's wife's father's child" at the base his mythical being is represented holding two salmon, above is the Raven, over the head of which are two thunderbirds, known as the slaves of the Raven, name[d] Kitz ah nook and Kitz ah Kake, at the top of the pole is a hawk flying.

The other pole belonging to the [__] represents a brown[?] bear at the base, above which is a hawk[?] connected to a raven[?].

Of old villages of which nothing remains, Vancouver mentions one of considerable size on a high detached rock off the southern extremity of Duke Island.

Thuwelut was on the west coast of Annette Island.

Sháa Nóow (Mountain fort) was on the southwest side of Revillagigedo Island.

Tongass Narrows originally belonged to the Cape Fox people, but was taken from them by the Taanta in the last century. Along its shores are numerous small clearings showing evidence of occupation, but in 1888 no people lived hereabouts, but camped near streams for the salmon fishing in the summer season. The names of the old villages ending in noow (fort) indicate that they were defensive points, but from their size they must have been only a house or two.

Noow Tlein (Big fort) was on the bluff just below Ketchikan

Heen ya ya nalth ka nu (Water around fort) was on a rock on the north bank of the Ketchikan stream near its mouth.

Tlákwaan Noow (Mother or old fort) was where the Ketchikan wharf stands[.] Klarta Noow [was] across from Ketchikan on Pennock Island.

The Taanta Kwáan traded at Port Simpson until the establishment of custom houses in Alaska. This brought them intermittently in contact with the Tsimshian, Nootka and Haida and resulted in much intermarriage and exchange of ideas and customs that made them more cosmopolitan in their habits. The practice of the Secret Societies of the Kwakuitl was thus introduced. The custom of erecting totem poles and artistic sense of these more southern people is shown in their workmanship.

***

T'AAKU KWÁAN

The T'aaku Kwáan take their name from the inlet and river given from the great run of king salmon (t'á) and nest (ku) — King Salmon nest tribe. Another version of the name given to me in an old story says that the inlet was named Goose nesting place, which contracted to T'aaku.* In early days, when the glaciers extended much farther, the river currents and tides carried the bergs to the narrow mouth leaving open water near shore where the geese assembled in great numbers.

Among an Interior tribe living about the headwaters of the T'aaku the seduction of the Chief's young wife divided the people and the family in fault left their home and followed down the river until brought to a halt by a great glacier spanning the narrow gully, but under which the swift current had cut a channel. Uncertain as to the passage, they set two slaves adrift in a canoe and in some days they returned on foot over the ice when all embarked and, emerging from the ice, came to a great body of comparatively still water that was made alive by (the shrill cries of) innumerable wild geese. They named the country accordingly from there and they took their own names accordingly.

They constitute one of the later Tlingit tribes, as the passage of the T'aaku was some generations after that of the Skeena, Nass and the Stikine, while the Chilkat and Hoonah tribes had been established long before this people came into existence. The majority of the families are of Athabascan stock and came from the country back of the headwaters of the Stikine and T'aaku while others came north through inland waterways. They have always maintained relations of this people with the people of the upper river and continual intermarriage with them has given them privileges of hunting in the interior. Notwithstanding this intimate relationship they have, like all other of the coast tribes, looked down on the Athabascans and have excluded them from the coast except under conditions that

---

* Editors note: This is the preferred interpretation. See Elizabeth Nyman and Jeff Leer, *Gágiwdul.át: Brought Forth to Reconfirm. The Legacy of a Taku River Clan*, 1993. Yukon Nation Language Center and Alaska Native Language Center.

placed the trade in their hands as middlemen. Unlike the more Southern Tlingit who wandered far and peopled the coast from Dixon Entrance to Prince William Sound, the T'aaḵu never got beyond the neighborhood of Taku Inlet.

Their country extended on the mainland shore from just below Juneau on Gastineau channel to the southern entrance point of Snettisham Bay, but then overlapping occurs with the S'aawdáan from the appearance of the S'itḵweidí family in both tribes. This bay was settled by this family that in part later removed to Holkam Bay and became the founders of the S'aawdáan Ḵwáan, but still claim certain rights in the original home on the eastern shore of Stevens Passage, [and] they claim the fringe of coast of Admiralty Island from Point Arden to Point Hugh. They extend much farther inland than other Tlingit and had villages on the Taku River almost to the forks.

The families are:

WOLF	RAVEN
Yanyeidí	Ḡaanax̱.ádi
Tsaat'ineidí	Ishkahittaan
S'itḵweidí	Kóoḵhittaan
Tooḵa.adi	Kayautdi [Gáaya.ádi?]

The Yanyeidí claim to have been the first to descend the Taku and settled along the mainland shore from the mouth of the river southward as far as Taku Harbor. They founded the village of Sik'nax̱ Aan Ḡeeyí (Grindstone Bay), and lay claim to certain fishing streams and hunting grounds in Snettisham. They have always held the first place of the Wolf phratry in this tribe.

The Tsaat'ineidi are of Athabascan stock in common with the Yanyeidí and the Tleintaan [L'eeneidí?] of the Aak'w Ḵwáan. From their scant records and movements, it seems more than likely that they are a branch of the latter people. They descended the T'aaḵu and crossing over Stephens Passage, settl[ing] on the northern shore of Admiralty Island at Tsaatehéeni (Behind the seals) [Youngs Bay] where many hair seal congregated among the floating bergs from Taku Inlet, and here they took their name. Owing to a quarrel with the Tleintaan they removed en masse to the mainland and joined the T'aa_ku _Kwáan where they are alone found and form but a small family.

The S'it_kweidi claim to have been the earliest settlers on Stephens Passage. They are of Athabascan origin and reached the coast by way of the Stikine, and migrated north, settling at Sit'_Geeyí (Glacier Bay) in Snettisham where some remained and joined this tribe while others removed to Holkam Bay and founded the S'aawdáan _Kwáan. They have always held the first place socially in both tribes.

The _Gaanax.ádi are of southern origin and, in an early migration from the Prince of Wales Island, reached Admiralty Island and lived with the Xootsidaaya _Kwáan until trouble with the Deisheetaan compelled them to leave, when they joined the T'aa_ku where they form the most important division of the Raven people.

The Ishkahittaan are an offshoot of the _Gaanax.ádi and while some claim that the division took place at Chilkat, it is much more probable that it occurred at T'aa_ku.

Of the three remaining families, extinct or nearly so, little is known. Kóo_khittaan are believed to have descended the Stikine. The Kahyahutdi [_Gaaya.ádi?] and the Too_ka.aádi followed the T'aa_ku to the coast. All of these people were of Athabascan stock and possibly were nearly related. None of them attained any importance and formed but small groups.

The earliest settlements were on the Taku and at and about Taku Inlet. In time they settled in the bays on the mainland to the southward as far as Snettisham and while they claimed the shore of Admiralty Island across Stephens Passage they had no villages there. The principal village at the head of Taku Harbor was named Sik'na_x sáank'i from the fish traps in the stream flowing from a lake back of the village. In 1869 there were ten houses and the remains of a stockade, and in 1882 there were eight large old houses in fair condition, but the establishment of Juneau had already altered all of the nearby Natives who, finding employment in the mines, had deserted their old villages and lived on the shore of Gastineau channel, returning to their villages for the winter feasts and ceremonies and by degrees the houses were allowed to fall to decay. After the establishment of a salmon cannery they returned to Taku Harbor and rebuilt the village on modern plans. In 1840, after the lease of southeastern Alaska to the Hudson Bay Company, they built a trading post here. Just within the southern entrance was [a] stockaded [village], the remains of which could be seen as late as 1882. Captain Richard Meade, in command of our Naval forces in Alaska in 1869, mentions a stockaded village of 12 houses just to the eastward of Point Salisbury at the head of Stephens Passage, but by 1882 this had wholly disappeared, one fishing house alone marking the site.

In 1888, those who lived about Juneau, together with others from the Inlet and River settlements and some connections from the Interior, found the village of T'aaku Aan (T'aaku Town) on the mainland shore just to the westward of Point Salisbury. The Sik'nax̱.ádi were the principal element in this movement, but were followed by the others who realized the inroads dissipation had made on their ranks from living in close contact with mining camps.

L'éiwu Aan (In the midst of sand) was an old village some twelve miles up the Taku River which has later been deserted.

S'ik Noow (Black Bear fort) was a fortified village some forty miles up the Taku which has likewise disappeared. Village and camp sites are visible in Taku and Limestone Inlets and Snettisham marked by berry bushes and fireweed.

The T'aaku, from continued intermarriage with the Interior tribes and their constant visits to there which often extended over seasons and even years, were less Tlingit in appearance and customs than other of the coast people, but notwithstanding this close relationship and association they were just as arbitrary in their methods of excluding their Interior neighbors from visiting or trading on the coast as all other Tlingit. After the establishment of Juneau, in the early summer, when the river was high, the upriver people came down with their furs and lived as guests with their coast relatives, but in trading with the stores they were carefully supervised by their hosts who took part in every transaction to their own advantage.

Before the advent of whites, the coast people traded for dressed caribou and moose skins and fur pelts for clothing, but after European ships appeared, this traffic was greatly promoted by the increased demand for furs, and the position of this tribe on one of the few Interior waterways increased their importance and wealth, but inevitably they never seemed to get away from their later Interior connection and were rather looked down on socially by the older Tlingits.

L'UKNAX̱.ÁDI

L'uknax̱.ádi (People of or belonging to the Coho Salmon Bay) claim to have come from the Tsimshian coast above the mouth of the Skeena and from the bay and to be of common stock with the G̱aanax̱.ádi. In very early times they crossed Dixon Entrance and lived with the Taantá Ḵwáan at Klinkwan. From there they moved northward through the outer island channels and settled just below Klawock at the mouth of a small stream that empties into a bay in the form of a halibut hook where many coho salmon gathered, and here they took their family name. The old chief Satán said that it was when living there that the trial of strength between the two chiefs Kish ka ta and Dukt'ootl' among the sea lions took place, which resulted in the death of the former and caused the separation that carried this family north to Cross Sound where they became a part of the Xunaa Ḵáawu and are mentioned in connection with the oldest lived places.

But they seem to have been of an adventurous disposition for from here they went to sea and following up the coast settled first at Nook hook heen. Either here or near here at Tah an [Ta.áan, Sleep Town] occurred the killing of the sleep spirit, an important event in the life of the family from which they take the bird crest Tah and name their houses accordingly. They continued northward and entering Dry Bay established themselves about the mouth of the Alsek and the inland waters leading to Yakutat and later pushed westward to the mouth of the Copper River which tradition says they named Giyaḵw Héeni (Copper water).

They traded with the far western people for native copper from which the highly prized shield-like plates were made, as well as knives, spears, arrow blades and ornaments, and from the Interior tribes of the Alsek, with whom they were the first of the coast people to come in contact, they procured moose and caribou hides so much in demand for clothing. After the destruction of the Glacier Bay villages by the great ice movement those remaining among the Xunaa removed to [Ḵohkei]kee.áan (In front of the damp ground town) at the head of Swanson Harbor on the mainland at the entrance of Icy Straits under Pt. Couverdon where the land is low and swampy. The decayed timbers of the old houses could still be seen in 1890. This was eventually a L'uknax̱.ádi village with few outsiders.

Towards the middle of the last century, possibly earlier, after the Kaagwaantaan movement to Sitka, all of this community followed and were incorporated in the Sitka Ḵwáan where they had four large communal houses and had a first place in social importance. In later years, since our occupation of Alaska, the villages about Dry Bay, the Alsek and the inland waters connecting with Yakutat, have been practically abandoned and the inhabitants have removed to the modern town at Yakutat. Kah harts ka an [Ḵahaatka.áan?] (between two hills) where they occupy the highest position.

They are much intermarried with the Kaagwaantaan and although decreased in population and wealth they continue to hold their place as the first of the Raven party.

They use the Raven crest almost to the exclusion of others but recognize the Coho salmon, the swan and the whale and in the chief's house at Yakutat the interior posts are carved to represent the sleep spirit, while at Sitka the principal house is named Ta Hít [or Kuta Hít?] (Sleep house).

The Dry Bay branch of the family claimed and used the frog crest, but in 1895 when the Sitka family exhibited it as a carved wood frog figure over the doorway of a new house, the Kiks.ádi demanded its immediate withdrawal and a fight would have ensued had not the authorities intervened. But beyond the mere display of the crest, which is the most honored among the Kiks.ádi, its display here had an ulterior significance as it proclaimed an unfulfilled obligation on the part of the latter family, and the taking of another crest was a public posting of a family debt that brought great shame to the debtor.

The facial painting of the dead was the design Yéil lú (Raven nose) an isosceles triangle with the apex at the bridge of the nose. the band extending across the chin in black. The same figure in red or black is used for feasts.

X'AT'KA.AAYÍ

X'at'ka.aayí (Island people) take their name from a peculiarly shaped pointed island in Dry Bay, where they first camped or built their houses, [and] where they separated from the L'uknax̲.ádi and proclaimed their independence. As they increased in numbers, they settled in several permanent villages about the delta of the Alsek. Kooth ache anelith to heen nock [?] and Kuze gun ke yar [?] on the Akwe River to the northward, [at] which they claimed a right to hunt sea otter as far south at Lituya Bay when they met the T'ak̲deintaan of the Xunaa K̲áawu and with whom they lived for a least a considerable portion of the year at Kaháakw Héeni (Fish egg water) some three miles north of Lituya which was sighted by La Perouse in 1786.

They came in contact with the Interior tribes of the upper Alsek and are said to have suffered severely in their constant wars with them. They must have separated from the main body at an early period as they are mentioned as inhabitants of some of the early Huna villages to which they came from the north and a family or two are found today at Gaaw T'ak Aan. Towards the middle of the last century [they] commenced to come to Sitka, first as winter visitors and later to settle where they built three communal houses, but even as late as 1895, as families, they would go north in summer to their salmon streams about Dry Bay and some would remain to hunt and trap through the year. As a clan they have never occupied a very important position although later [they became] much intermarried with Kaagwaantaan.

They use but two crests, restricting themselves almost exclusively to the Raven and Coho salmon. The principal chief of the Sitka branch wears, upon ceremonial occasions, a woven spruce root hat with superimposed cylinders ornamented in front with the head of a raven in wood and painted in like design. His name and that of his house was of the coho salmon and carvings of the same were attached to the interior house posts. The family names were generally of the Raven and the salmon. The facial painting of the dead is in the design Héen Xokatsee Istee (water dropping down) to commemorate the giving of fresh water to the world by the Raven, and in the general family painting of the "Raven's nose" with the addition of the color around both eyes.

SIK'NA̲X.ÁDI

The Sik'na̲x.ádi/People of Sik'na̲x (Limestone Inlet on Stephens Passage) are so named from the geological formation, the rock which the Natives used as a whetstone.

They are of Athabascan stock, and as one people with the Naanya.aayí lived about the head waters of the Stikine and the Taku rivers. Together they came down the Taku to the coast where they separated. The Naanya.aayí going south to Wrangell, the Sik'na̲x.ádi settling around the Coast Taku, where they lived for some time, but through continued feuds and warfare with the Auk K̲wáan they were so worsted that they migrated south in a body and settled among the Stikine and resumed their close relations with the Naanya.aayí and built their houses alongside of them on the small highwater island in the inner harbor at Wrangell. Their crests are the Wolf, Brown Bear, Murrelet, a water bug known as Suck-nar and the Aaank' which as a cane was captured in war from the Tsimshians and is represented on a totem pole in front of the chief's house as a man seated with knees drawn unto the chin and on his head a ceremonial hat surmounted [by] superimposed cylinders. The facial painting is the wolf's ears and the brown bear's ears. For war the face was painted to represent a rock, Khon ghit leo, on the upper Stikhine river. The following legend was given to me by the chief of the clan.

"In early days the Sik'na̲x.ádi steamed and spread their partly made canoes on the shore of a bight just below Shustale Toon

[?] which was named York-tahk-heen-har-an [Yakw Tak Héen Aan ?] (Canoe boiling water country). All canoes were spread amidships by boiling in the canoe with heated stones where stretchers were inserted.

It was here during a famine that the chief was camped with his two wives, his nephew and the latter's grandmother. The nephew Ka-tcha-ta (lazy man) was considered worthless and the old woman useless, so when the others set out on quest of food they were left to starve. However, the younger of the wives buried a salmon in the ashes of the fire. Upon this they lived for a few days. When it was finished the boy gave up and lay down to die. As he slept he thought that a rock called him but upon waking he saw no one. Again the rock called and he saw it was the loon. That told him to carve a killer whale from cedar and put it in the water. This he did, where the wooden figure became alive, and as his work drove the seal, eulachon and all sea life shoreward, for the loon gave him supernatural power over both animal and fish life. Then he became a great shaman. He built a large house for his grandmother, supplying her with all kinds of food. In the meantime, the uncle, believing them dead, sent slaves to cremate them, but to their surprise, however, they saw the new house, and the grandmother had been transformed into a young woman. They were feasted with all kinds of food, but were not permitted to take anything away. However, one of them secreted some eulachon for a sick child. When the child was fed at night it cried for more until the chief's suspicions were aroused. Finally, they confessed to him that the nephew was alive and had become very powerful. The chief and all of his followers dressed in ceremonial garb and set out to visit him. When they arrived he told the grandmother to beat the great box drum, which she did, by nodding her head towards it. It made such a great noise that the sea animals and fish came swiftly shoreward, and cast themselves on the beach. A great feast was held. The women sold their children to him for food. This apparently was at one time the accepted custom during famine. It was practiced by the Kitikshaan of the Upper Skeena River, who gave their children to the Nishka [in return] for food, the latter selling them as slaves to the Haida. The elder wife, to show her contrition for her hard heartedness in the past, cut her face and rubbed moss in the wounds. He married the younger wife who had befriended him and he became a very powerful chief of the Sik'na x̱.ádi and his name has always remained in this family.

B. THE TRADITIONAL TLINGIT MAP & TRIBAL LIST PROJECT

Administrative support: Sealaska Heritage Foundation, the Sitka Tribe of Alaska, Alaska Native Brotherhood Camp 2, Alaska Federation of Natives and the University of Alaska Southeast. Grant funding: the National Science Foundation, Annenberg Foundation, Alaska Native Programs/University of Alaska Fairbanks and Klukwan Heritage Foundation.

This list of Tlingit tribes, clans and clan houses was compiled and reconstructed by Andrew Hope, III. The list is by no means final. It is a work in progress. The following sources were used to develop the list:

1. Unpublished "genealogical papers," by Louis Shotridge (n.d.)

2. The unpublished manuscript: "History of Tlingit Tribes and Clans, by George Emmons (n.d.)

3. The unpublished list of "Tlingit Tribe, Clan, and House Group Names," by Jeff Leer (1985)

4. *Social Structure and Social Life of the Tlingit Alaskan,* by Ronald Olson (1967)

5. *Social Conditions, Beliefs, and Linguistic Relationship of the Tlingit Indians,* by John Swanton (1970 [1908])

6. An unpublished list of Angoon clan houses by Lydia George (1967)

7. *My Old People Say,* by Catherine McClellan (1975)

8. Conversations Andrew Hope had with the following individuals, some of whom have since passed into the spirit world: Harry Bremner Sr., George Davis, Henry Davis, Sr., Nora Dauenhauer, Forrest DeWitt, Sr., Albert Frank, Sr., Matthew Fred, Sr., Jimmie George, Sr., Lydia George, Paul Jackson, Mark Jacobs, George James, George Jim, Sr., George John, Sr., Andrew P. Johnson, William Nelson, Sr., Charlie Olson, William Paul, Sr., Tom Ukas, Jimmy Williams, Sr., Robert Zuboff

9. Kake names were compiled by: Ruth Demmert, Mike Jackson, Dawn Skee' Jackson and Topsy Johnson.

10. The list was revised in July 1997 in Sitka by Tlingit Language Workshop participants, including: Bessie Cooley, Lonnie Hotch, Jennie Lindoff, Roby Littlefield, Nellie Lord, Ethel Makinen, Al McKinley, Emma Sam, Esther Shea, Margaret Stevens, Carol Williams.

G̲ALYÁX̲ K̲WÁAN:
YAKATAGA-CONTROLLER BAY AREA
SALMON STREAM TRIBE

RAVEN MOIETY

G̲aanax̲.ádi
K̲oosk'eidí
Kwáashk'i K̲wáan
Tuk̲yeidí

WOLF/EAGLE MOIETY

Kaagwaantaan
Jishk̲weidí

LAAX̲AAYÍK K̲WÁAN: YAKUTAT AREA
NEAR THE ICE PEOPLE

RAVEN MOIETY

L'uknax̲.ádi
  Shaa Hít
  (MOUNTAIN HOUSE-
    for Mt. Fairweather)
  Daginaa Hít
  (FAR OUT IN THE SEA
    HOUSE)
  Eech Hít 1
  (REEF HOUSE 1)
  Eech Hít 2
  (REEF HOUSE 2-
    located at Situk River)
Kwaashk'i K̲wáan
  Aanyuwaa Hít
  (IN FRONT OF TOWN
    HOUSE)
  Tsisk'w Hít
  (OWL HOUSE)
  Dís Hít
  (MOON HOUSE)
  Yéil S'aagi Hít
  (RAVEN'S BONES
    HOUSE)
  Noow Hít
  (FORT HOUSE)
  Shaa Hít
  (MOUNTAIN HOUSE—
    for Mt. St. Elias)

WOLF/EAGLE MOIETY

Kaagwaantaan
  Gooch X̲aay Hít
  (WOLF STEAM BATH
    HOUSE)
Lk̲uweidi
Teik̲weidí
  Xeitl Hít
  (THUNDERBIRD
    HOUSE 2)
  Gijook Hít
  (GOLDEN EAGLE
    HOUSE)
  Gaaw Hít (DRUM
    HOUSE)
  K'atx̲aan Hít
  (MAN WHO ACTED
    LIKE A WOMAN
    HOUSE)
  Tóos' Hít (SHARK
    HOUSE)
  Xóots Hít
  (BROWN BEAR HOUSE)
Dagisdinaa
  Xeitl Hít
  (THUNDERBIRD
    HOUSE 1)

GUNAAXOO KWÁAN: DRY BAY
AMONG THE ATHABASCANS TRIBE

RAVEN MOIETY

X'at'ka.aayí
Koosk'eidí
   Xaas Hít (COW HOUSE)
L'uknax.ádi
   Xíxch'i Hít
   (FROG HOUSE)
Lukaax.ádi
   Shaka Hít
   (CANOE PROW HOUSE)

WOLF/EAGLE MOIETY

Dagisdinaa

JILKAAT KWÁAN: KLUKWAN
CHILKAT TRIBE

RAVEN MOIETY

Gaanaxteidí
   X'áakw Hít
   (FRESHWATER MARKED
     SOCKEYE HOUSE)
   Yaay Hít
   (WHALE HOUSE)
   X'aak Hít
   (GULLY OR RAVINE HOUSE)
   Kutis' Hít
   (LOOKING OUT HOUSE)
   Xíxch'i Hít
   (FROG HOUSE)
   Ishka Hít
   (HOUSE ON THE SALMON
     HOLE IN THE RIVER)
Lukaax.ádi
Naach'ooneidí
Noowshaka.aayí

WOLF/EAGLE MOIETY

Kaagwaantaan
   Gooch Hít (WOLF HOUSE)
   Kéet Hít
   (KILLER WHALE HOUSE)
   Ligooshi Hít
   (KILLER WHALE DORSAL FIN
     HOUSE)
Dagisdinaa
   Xeitl Hít
   (THUNDERBIRD HOUSE)
   Shis'gi Hít
   (SAPLING HOUSE)
Dakl'aweidí
   Ch'eet Hít
   (MURRELET HOUSE)
   Tleilu Hít (MOTH HOUSE)
   Kéet Gooshi Hít
   (KILLER WHALE DORSAL FIN
     HOUSE)
   Kéet Kwáani Hít
   (KILLER WHALE PEOPLE HOUSE)
   Kéet L'oót'i Hít
   (KILLER WHALE TONGUE
     HOUSE)
   Kéet Déx'i Hít
   (KILLER WHALE BACKBONE
     HOUSE)

JILKOOT KWÁAN: HAINES
CHILKOOT TRIBE

RAVEN MOIETY

Lukaax.ádi
  Yéil Hít
  (RAVEN HOUSE)
  Yéil Kiji Hít
  (RAVEN'S WING
  HOUSE)
  Shaa Hít
  (MOUNTAIN HOUSE)
  Kooshdaa Hít
  (LAND OTTER HOUSE)
  Geisán Hít
  (MT. RIPINSKY HOUSE)

WOLF/EAGLE MOIETY

Shangukeidí
  Kaawdliyaayi Hít
  (HOUSE LOWERED FROM
  THE SUN)
Kaagwaantaan
  Xóots Hít
  (BROWN BEAR
  HOUSE)
  Ch'áak' Hít
  (EAGLE HOUSE)
  Kaawagaani Hít
  (BURNT HOUSE)

XUNAA KWÁAN a.k.a. KÁAWU: HOONAH
TRIBE OR PEOPLE FROM THE DIRECTION OF
THE NORTHWIND

RAVEN MOIETY

T'akdeintaan
  T'akdein Hít
  (T'AKDEIN HOUSE)
  X'áakw Hít
  (FRESHWATER MARKED
  COHO HOUSE)
  X'áakw Yádi Hít
  (SMALL FRESHWATER
  SOCKEYE HOUSE)
  Yéil Kúdi Hít
  (RAVEN'S NEST HOUSE)
  Yéil Hít (RAVEN HOUSE)
  Yáay Hít (WHALE HOUSE)
  K'óox Dísi Hít
  (MARTEN MOON HOUSE)
  Teet Hít
  (WAVE HOUSE)
  Kaa Shaayi Hít
  (MAN'S HEAD HOUSE)
  Tax' Hít (SNAIL HOUSE)
Koosk'eidí
  Xaas Hít
  (COW HOUSE)
Gaanax.ádi
  Gaanaxaa Hít
  (GAANAXAA HOUSE)

WOLF/EAGLE MOIETY

Wooshkeetaan
  Wooshdaa Hít
  (OVER ALL HOUSE)
  Tóos' Déx'i Hít
  (SHARK BACKBONE HOUSE)
  Noow Hít
  (FORT HOUSE)
Chookaneidí
  Naanaa Hít
  (UP THE BAY HOUSE)
  Xáatl Hít
  (ICEBERG HOUSE)
  Xóots Saagi Hít
  (BROWN BEAR'S NEST HOUSE)
  Wandaa Hít
  (AROUND THE EDGE HOUSE)
  Xóots Hít
  (BROWN BEAR HOUSE)
  Yan Wulihashi Hít
  (DRIFTED ASHORE HOUSE)
  Aan Eegayaak Hít
  (ICEBERG ON THE BEACH HOUSE)
  Shux'aa Xaay Hít
  (FIRST YELLOW CEDAR HOUSE)
Kadakw.ádi
  Xáay Hít
  (YELLOW CEDAR HOUSE)
Kaagwaantaan
  Xóots Kúdi Hít
  (BROWN BEAR'S NEST HOUSE)

T'AAKU KWÁAN: TAKU
GEESE FLOOD UPRIVER TRIBE

RAVEN MOIETY

Gaanax.ádi
  Ishka Hít
  (SALMON HOLE HOUSE)
  Yanwulihashi Hít
  (DRIFTED ASHORE HOUSE)
  Yéil Hít (RAVEN HOUSE)
Ishkahittaan
Kookhittaan
Tooka.ádi

WOLF/EAGLE MOIETY

Yanyeidí
  Ch'aal' Hít
  (WILLOW HOUSE)
Tsaateeneidí
  Xóots Hít
  (BROWN BEAR HOUSE)
Yayuwaa Hít
  (BETWEEN THE RIVER
  FORK HOUSE)
S'eet'kweidí

DEISLEEN KWÁAN: TESLIN
BIG SINEW TRIBE

RAVEN MOIETY

Ishkeetaan
Kookhittaan
Deisheetaan

WOLF/EAGLE MOIETY

Dakl'aweidí
Yanyeidí

ÁA TLEIN KWÁAN: ATLIN
BIG LAKE TRIBE

RAVEN MOIETY

Ishkeetaan
Kookhittaan
  Xaas Hít
  (COW HOUSE)
Deisheetaan

WOLF/EAGLE MOIETY

Yanyeidí
  Yayuwaa Hít
  (BETWEEN THE RIVER
  FORK HOUSE)
Dakl'aweidí

AAK'W KWÁAN: AUKE BAY
SMALL LAKE TRIBE

RAVEN MOIETY
L'eeneidí
  Gaatáa Hít (TRAP HOUSE)
  Téel' Hít (DOG SALMON HOUSE)
  Yaxte Hít (BIG DIPPER HOUSE)
L'uknax.ádi
  L'ook Hít (COHO SALMON HOUSE)
Gaanax.ádi
  Gaanaxaa Hít (GAANAXAA HOUSE)
  Yéil Hít (RAVEN HOUSE)

WOLF/EAGLE MOIETY
Wooshkeetaan
  Gunakadeit Hít (SEA MONSTER HOUSE)
  Hít Tlein (BIG HOUSE)
  Noow Hít (FORT HOUSE)
  Tóos' Hít (SHARK HOUSE)
  Xeitl Hít (THUNDER HOUSE)
  Xóots Hít (BROWN BEAR HOUSE)

S'AWDAAN KWÁAN: SUMDUM
DUNGENESS CRAB TOWN TRIBE

RAVEN MOIETY
?

WOLF/EAGLE MOIETY
S'eet'kweidí
  Sit' Hít (GLACIER HOUSE)
  S'eek Hít (BLACK BEAR HOUSE)

XUTSNOOWÚ ḴWÁAN: ANGOON
BROWN BEAR FORT, a.k.a.:
XUDZIDAA ḴWÁAN — BURNT WOOD TRIBE

RAVEN MOIETY

Deisheetaan
  Dáanaa Hít
  (SILVER HOUSE)
  Deishú Hít
  (END OF THE ROAD HOUSE)
  Góon Hít
  (FRESHWATER SPRING HOUSE)
  Shdéen Hít
  (STEEL HOUSE)
  Tuḵka Hít
  (NEEDLEFISH HOUSE)
  Yéil Hít
  (RAVEN HOUSE)
  Yéil S'aagi Hít
  (RAVEN'S BONES HOUSE)
Ḵak'weidí
  Kaḵáak'w Hít
  (BASKET BAY ARCH HOUSE)
L'eeneidí
  Aanx̱'aak Hít
  (CENTRAL HOUSE)
  Yanxoon Hít
  (LOG JAM HOUSE)

WOLF/EAGLE MOIETY

Daḵl'aweidí
  Kéet Hít
  (KILLER WHALE HOUSE)
  A.K.A. WOOCH DAKÁDIN HÍT (HOUSE FACING AWAY FROM OTHERS)
  Yaa Ayaanasnaḵ Kéet Hít
  (KILLER WHALE CHASING A SEAL HOUSE)
  Kéet Ooxú Hít
  (KILLER WHALE'S TOOTH HOUSE)
Teiḵweidí
  Shaanax̱ Hít
  (VALLEY HOUSE)
  Xóots Hít
  (BROWN BEAR HOUSE)
Wooshkeetaan
  Noow Hít (FORT HOUSE)
  Noow Shaka Hít
  (HEAD FORT HOUSE)
  Xóots Kúdi Hít
  (BROWN BEAR'S NEST HOUSE)

KEEX̱' K̲WÁAN: KAKE
THE OPENING OF THE DAY (DAWN) TRIBE
a.k.a. THE TOWN THAT NEVER SLEEPS

RAVEN MOIETY

K̲aach.ádi
  X̱'áakw Hít
  (FRESHWATER MARKED
   SOCKEYE HOUSE)
  K̲utis' Hít
  (LOOKING OUT TO SEA
   HOUSE)
Suk̲teeneidí
  Aanx̱'aak Hít
  (MIDDLE OF TOWN HOUSE)
  Shaa Hít
  (MOUNTAIN HOUSE)
  Tax̱' Hít (SNAIL HOUSE)
  Wandaa Hít
  (WOODEN ARMOR HOUSE)
  Yéik Hít (SPIRIT HOUSE)
Teeyineidí
  Kóoshdaa Hít
  (LAND OTTER HOUSE)
  Teey Hít
  (CEDAR BARK HOUSE)
X̱'alchaneidí

WOLF/EAGLE MOIETY

Tsaagweidí
  Aan Yakawlitseix̱i Hít
  (THE HOUSE THAT ANCHORED
   THE VILLAGE)
  Tóos' Hít
  (SHARK HOUSE)
  X̱aay Hít
  (YELLOW CEDAR HOUSE)
Wooshkeetaan
  Tóos' Hít (SHARK HOUSE)
  Noow Hít (FORT HOUSE)
Shangukeidí
  Kóok Hít
  (BOX HOUSE)
Nees.ádi
  Kéet Gooshí Hít
  (KILLER WHALE FIN HOUSE)
Was'ineidí
  Tax̱' Hít
  (PLATFORM OR BENCH HOUSE)

SHEEY AT`IKÁ (a.k.a. SHEET'KÁ) ꞰWÁAN: SITKA
OUTSIDE EDGE OF A BRANCH TRIBE

RAVEN MOIETY

Kiks.ádi
 At.uwaxiji Hít
 (STRONG HOUSE)
 Gagaan Hít (SUN HOUSE)
 Kaxátjaa Hít
 (JUMPING HERRING HOUSE)
 Noowtu Hít
 (INSIDE THE FORT HOUSE)
 Noow Daganyaa Hít
 (OUTSIDE THE FORT HOUSE)
 S'é Hít (CLAY HOUSE)
 Shdéen Hít
 (STEEL HOUSE)
 Tináa Hít
 (COPPER SHIELD HOUSE)
 X'aaká Hít
 (POINT HOUSE)
Watineidí
Ꞣoosk'eidí
 Xaas Hít (COW HOUSE)
L'uknax.ádi
 Daginaa Hít (OUT IN THE
 OCEAN SALMON BOX
 HOUSE)
 Ꞣuta Hít (SLEEP HOUSE)
 L'ook Hít Tlein
 (BIG COHO HOUSE)
 L'ook Hít Yádi
 (SMALL COHO HOUSE)
 Shgat.aayi Hít
 (HOUSE NAMED FOR CREEK
 NEAR YAKUTAT)
 Taan Hít
 (SEA LION HOUSE)
 Xinaa Hít
 (HOUSE AT THE LOWER END
 OF TOWN)
 Xinaa Hít 2
 (HOUSE AT THE LOWER END
 OF TOWN)
 Xíxch'i Hít
 (FROG HOUSE)
 Yáay Hít (WHALE HOUSE)
T'aꞣdeintaan
 Danakoo Hít
 (DANAKOO HOUSE)
X'at'ka.aayí
 Kayaashka Hít
 (PLATFORM HOUSE)
 L'ook Hít (COHO HOUSE)

WOLF/EAGLE MOIETY

Kaagwaantaan
 Aanyádi Hít
 (NOBILITY HOUSE)
 Eech Hít (REEF HOUSE)
 Ch'áak' Hít (EAGLE HOUSE)
 Ch'áak' Kúdi Hít
 (EAGLE'S NEST HOUSE)
 Ch'eet Hít (MURRELET
 HOUSE)
 Cháatl Hít (HALIBUT HOUSE)
 Déix X'awool Hít
 (HOUSE WITH TWO DOORS)
 Gayéis' Hít (IRON HOUSE)
 Gooch Hít (WOLF HOUSE)
 Kutxayanahá Hít
 (STAR HOUSE)
 Heenka Hít
 (HOUSE ON THE WATER)
 Xóots Hít
 (BROWN BEAR HOUSE)
 Kaawagaani Hít
 (BURNED HOUSE)
 Ꞣuháada Hít
 (FISH-CHASING STICK HOUSE)
Ꞣookhittaan
 Tóos' Hít (SHARK HOUSE)
 Ꞣóok Hít (BOX HOUSE)
 Kutis' Hít
 (LOOKING OUT TO SEA HOUSE)
 Tl'aadein Hít
 (STANDING SIDEWAYS HOUSE)
Chookaneidí
 Xaatl Hít
 (ICEBERG HOUSE)
 Aan Eegayaak Hít
 (ICEBERG ON THE BEACH HOUSE)
Wooshkeetaan
 Noow Hít (FORT HOUSE)
X'ax'ahittaan
 X'ax'a Hít (CLIFF HOUSE)

KOOYU ḴWÁAN: KUIU ISLAND
STOMACH TRIBE

RAVEN MOIETY
Kooyu.eidí
Ḵutxayanahá Hít
(STAR HOUSE)
Xík Hít (PUFFIN
HOUSE)

WOLF/EAGLE MOIETY
Naasteidí
Ch'eet Hít
(MURRELET HOUSE)
Kóon Hít
(FLICKER HOUSE)
Deikee Noow Hít
(FAR OUT FORT HOUSE)

SHTAX'HÉEN ḴWÁAN: WRANGELL
BITTER WATER TRIBE

RAVEN MOIETY
Ḵaach.ádi
Náalx Hít
(HALIBUT HOUSE)
Xíxch'i Hít (FROG HOUSE)
Alḵaa Hít
(GAMBLING HOUSE)
Gaach Hít
(RUG OR MAT HOUSE)
Kaawdliyaayi Hít
(HOUSE LOWERED FROM THE SKY)
Yáay Hít (WHALE HOUSE)
Kaasx'agweidí
Xeitl Hít
(THUNDERBIRD HOUSE)
Tl'aadein Hít
(STANDING SIDEWAYS HOUSE)
Xíxch'i Xaayí Hít
(FROG'S DEN HOUSE)
Taan Hít
(SEA LION HOUSE)
Kiks.ádi
Gagaan Hít (SUN HOUSE)
Tax' Hít (SNAIL HOUSE)
Xíxch'i Hít
(FROG HOUSE)
Taalḵweidí
Shaa Hít
(MOUNTAIN HOUSE)
Kaxkuyendu Aa Hít
(NAME OF WATER SPIRIT
THAT LḴAAYAAK'W KILLED)
Gíl' Hít (CLIFF HOUSE)
Teeyhíttaan
Teey Hít (BARK HOUSE)

WOLF/EAGLE MOIETY
Kayaashkeiditaan
Kéet Hít
(KILLER WHALE HOUSE)
Kayaashka Hít
(PLATFORM HOUSE)
Naanyaa.aayí
X'atgu Hít
(DOGFISH HOUSE)
X'atgu Naasí Hít
(DOGFISH INTESTINE HOUSE)
Kóok Hít
(BOX HOUSE)
Hít Tlein
(BIG HOUSE)
Tatóok Hít
(CAVE HOUSE)
Chéx'i Hít
(SHADOW HOUSE)
Aan Shooka Hít
(HOUSE AT THE FAR END OF THE
OLD VILLAGE)
Sik'nax.ádi
X'aan Hít
(RED CLAY OR FIRE HOUSE)
Ank'w Hít
(TSIMSHIAN CANE HOUSE)
Xook'eidí
Shdéen Hít
(STEEL HOUSE)
Aandaa Óonaa Hít
(CANNON HOUSE)

TAANT'A ḴWÁAN: KETCHIKAN
SEA LION TRIBE

RAVEN MOIETY

Gaanax.ádi
  Gijook Hít
  (GOLDEN EAGLE HOUSE)
  Ḵutis' Hít
  (LOOKING OUT TO SEA
  HOUSE)
  Noow Hít (FORT HOUSE)
  S'áx Hít
  (STARFISH HOUSE)
  X'aagóon Hít
  (NARROW POINT HOUSE)
  Xaas Hít (COW HOUSE)
  Yáay Hít (WHALE HOUSE)
  Yan Wulihashi Hít
  (DRIFTED ASHORE HOUSE)

WOLF/EAGLE MOIETY

Teiḵweidí
  Kaats' Hít
  (HOUSE OF KAATS'- man who
  married the bear)
  Shaanax Hít
  (VALLEY HOUSE)
  Wandaa Hít
  (AROUND THE EDGE HOUSE)
  Xóots Hít
  (BROWN BEAR HOUSE)
Daḵl'aweidí
  Kéet Hít
  (KILLER WHALE HOUSE)
  Kóon Hít
  (FLICKER HOUSE)

TAḴJIK'AAN ḴWÁAN: PRINCE OF WALES
COAST TOWN TRIBE

RAVEN MOIETY

Gaanax.ádi
  Yan Wulihashi Hít
  (DRIFTED ASHORE HOUSE)
L'eeneidí
  Téel' Hít
  (DOG SALMON HOUSE)
  Téel' Yádi Hít
  (SMALL DOG SALMON
  HOUSE)
Taakw.aaneidí
  Taan Hít
  (SEA LION HOUSE)
Teeyneidí
  Gaaxka Hít
  (GAAXKA HOUSE)
  Héenka Hít
  (ON THE WATER HOUSE)
  S'ax Hít
  (STARFISH HOUSE)
  Yéil Hít
  (RAVEN HOUSE)
  Yéil Yadi Hít
  (SMALL RAVEN HOUSE)

WOLF/EAGLE MOIETY

Kaax'oos.hittaan
  Kaa X'oos Hít
  (MAN'S FOOT HOUSE)
Naasteidí
  Deikee Noow Hít
  (FAR OUT FORT HOUSE)
Shangukeidí
  Ch'áak' Hít
  (EAGLE HOUSE)
  Gooch Hít
  (WOLF HOUSE)
  Tsisk'w Hít
  (OWL HOUSE)
  X'atgu Hít
  (DOGFISH HOUSE)
Teiḵweidí
  Saanyaa Hít
  (SOUTHEAST HOUSE)

HINYAA K̲WÁAN: KLAWOCK
TRIBE FROM ACROSS THE WATER

RAVEN MOIETY

K'óoxeeneidí
  K'óox Hít
  (MARTEN HOUSE)
Taakw.aaneidí
  Yáay Hít (WHALE HOUSE)
Teeyneidí
  Yéil Hít (RAVEN HOUSE)
  Yan Wulihashi Hít
  (HOUSE DRIFTED ASHORE)
  Teey Hít (BARK HOUSE)

WOLF/EAGLE MOIETY

K̲aax̲'oos.hittaan
  Kaa X̲'oos Hít
  (MAN'S FOOT HOUSE)
  Tsisk'w Hít
  (OWL HOUSE)
Shangukeidí
  G̲unakadeit Hít
  (SEA MONSTER HOUSE)
  Xóots Hít
  (BROWN BEAR HOUSE)
Lk̲uweidí

SANYAA K̲WÁAN: CAPE FOX
SECURE IN RETREAT, LIKE A FOX IN ITS DEN/
SOUTHEAST TRIBE

RAVEN MOIETY

Kiks.ádi
  Wéix̲' Hít
  (BULLHEAD HOUSE)

WOLF/EAGLE MOIETY

Neix̲.ádi
  Ch'áak' Hít
  (EAGLE HOUSE)
  Ch'áak' X̲'oosi Hít
  (EAGLE FOOT HOUSE)
  S'igeidí X̲aayi Hít
  (BEAVER LODGE HOUSE)
  Ch'áak' Kúdi Hít
  (EAGLE NEST HOUSE)
  Ch'áak' K̲oowú Hít
  (EAGLE FAN-TAIL HOUSE)
  Chaatl Hít
  (HALIBUT HOUSE)
  X'éix̲ Hít
  (KING CRAB HOUSE)
  X̲eet' Hít
  (GIANT CLAM HOUSE)
Teik̲weidí
  Xóots K̲oowu Hít
  (BROWN BEAR'S DEN HOUSE)
  Kaats' Hít
  (HOUSE OF KAATS'— man who
  married the bear)
  G̲ooch Hít
  (WOLF HOUSE)